ANIMALS IN WAR

Jilly Cooper

ANIMALS IN WAR

HEINEMANN: LONDON

IN WAR

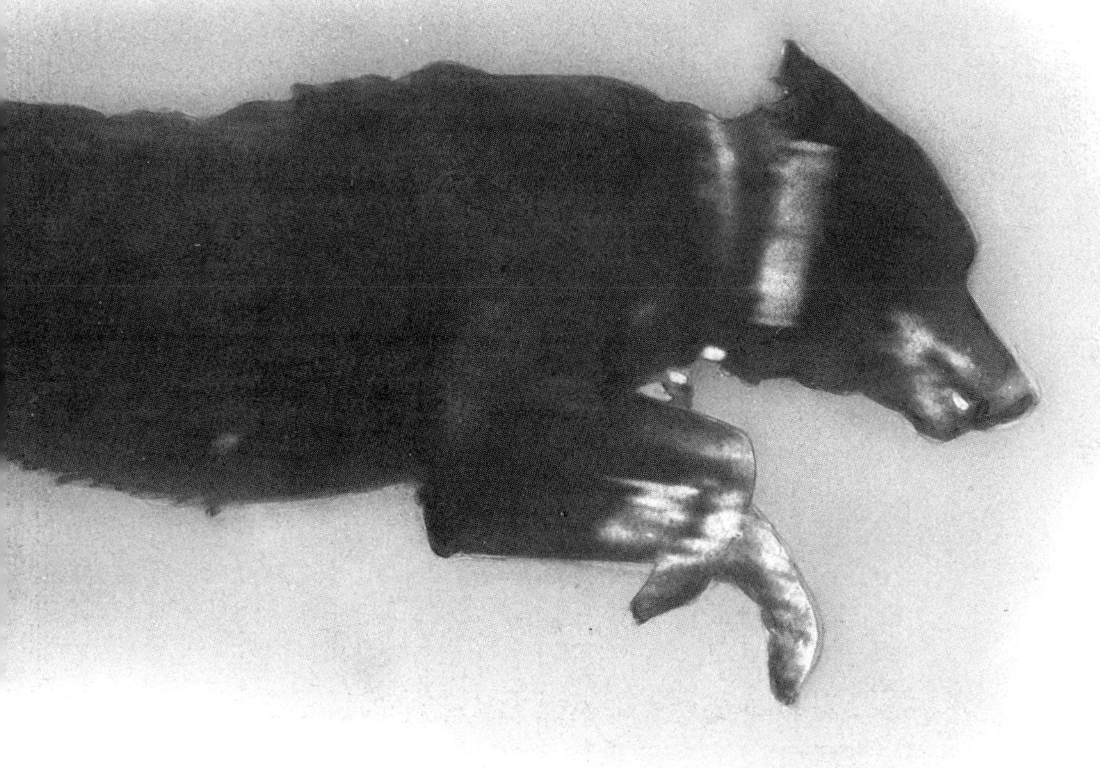

Nonfiction by the same author

Work and Wedlock
Superman and Superman
Jolly Super
Jolly Super Too
Jolly Superlative
Superjilly
Supercooper
Class
The British in Love
Intelligent and Loyal
Jolly Marsupial

WILLIAM HEINEMANN LTD
10 Upper Grosvenor Street, London W1X 9PA
LONDON MELBOURNE TORONTO JOHANNESBURG AUCKLAND

First published 1983
SBN 434 14370 7

Designed by Harry Green

Phototypeset in Linotron Garamond by Tradespools Ltd., Frome, Somerset
Printed and bound by Richard Clay (The Chaucer Press) Ltd., Bungay, Suffolk

To Leo

Contents

Author's Note 8

Introduction 10

My Kingdom for a Horse 12

Goodbye, old Man 28

The Golden Tail 54

Homer Sweet Homer 72

The Camel 84

The Mule 96

The Elephant 110

The Home Front 120

Mascots 134

The Hall of Fame 148

All Creatures Great and Small 154

Bibliography 164

Index 165

Author's Note

I am extremely grateful to the people who have helped me with this book. Heading the list must be the staff of the Imperial War Museum, including Dr Christopher Dowling and Angela Godwin, the Keeper and Deputy Keeper of the Department of Education and Publications, who thought up the idea in the first place, and were continually kind, encouraging and unstinting with their time and ideas; and secondly Dr Gwyn Bayliss, Keeper of the Department of Printed Books, who fell over backwards to let me have access to his books at all times. I would also like to thank the staff of Dr Dowling's department who spent so much time laboriously photostatting documents, and digging out photographs – marked 'IWM' where they appear – and to the museum warders who so cheerfully guided me round the museum on the numerous occasions when I got lost. (In the case of photographs with no attribution, the copyright holder is unknown though prints may be in the archives of the Imperial War Museum.)

I also owe a particular debt of gratitude to J.M.

Brereton, whose touching and beautifully written book, *The Horse in War*, was a constant inspiration to me when I wrote the two chapters about the horse; and to Henry Harris, who drew my attention to that wonderfully funny volume, *Mascots and Pets of the Regiments* by Major T.J. Edwards. Nor would this book have been written without help from the various histories of the P.D.S.A. and the R.S.P.C.A., and the official histories in both wars of the R.A.V.C.

I should like to offer a tremendous thanks to Lt.-Col. Keith Morgan Jones of the R.A.V.C. who not only entertained me most splendidly at their headquarters at Melton Mowbray, but also lent me every help while I was writing the book. My particular thanks also go to Jane Tebb and Olive Martyn of the R.S.P.C.A. and Clarissa Baldwin of the Canine Defence League who all provided me with excellent material, as did Mrs L.V. Travis, editor of that splendidly august journal: *The British Mule Society Magazine*.

May I also express my gratitude to all those readers of *The Times* and the *Daily Telegraph* who so promptly and generously answered my advertisement for stories of animals in war, and to Tonie and Valmai Holt for giving me the run of their magnificent postcard collection. I must thank Beryl Hill too for impeccably typing the manuscript, and David Godwin and Louise Bloomfield for editing it.

Above all, however, I am grateful to my own household: Claudia Wolfers, who dealt with the correspondence, and who with Stanley and Vivian Hicks, looked after me, and made it possible, just after we moved house to Gloucestershire, for me to isolate myself from the packing chests and the burst pipes, and to finish the book.

It only remains for me to thank my husband, Leo Cooper, whose photographic contributions to the book are marked 'LC'. By his vision, kindness, wide knowledge of military matters, and sense of humour, he is really the only begetter.

Introduction

One of the proudest moments of my life was when Dr Christopher Dowling of the Imperial War Museum asked me to write a book about the role animals have played in war to coincide with an exhibition on the same subject, which the Museum were planning to stage in the summer of 1983. For a dizzy moment, like the clown asked to play Hamlet, I felt I was being taken seriously as a writer.

It was only when I started work that I realised how singularly ill-equipped I was to write this book. For a start, I knew very little about *military* history. Being married to a military history publisher, Leo Cooper, for twenty-one years, has been rather like working in a sweet shop. I soon developed a complete block about the subject, and out of the 400 military books he has published, I had shamefully to confess I had read less than half a dozen. As a woman, I suspect I am not alone in having this block. In the same way that some men spurn novels, particularly romantic fiction, women tend to avoid war books, as being an exclusively guts-and-glory male province.

Having given up geography at twelve and history at seventeen (and being at a school where history stopped abruptly with Queen Victoria), I began writing from a position of total ignorance. I kept getting the First and Second World Wars dreadfully mixed up. How very inconsiderate, for example, of the Italians to have been our allies in the First World War, and not the Second. Geography posed even more of a problem, and the house rang with wails of 'Where the hell's Mesopotamia?' and 'Whatever happened to Salonika?'

Apart from getting my Salonika's in a twist, nothing had prepared me for the horror of the subject matter. I had no idea that eight million horses died in the Great War – imagine a capacity crowd at Wembley on Cup Final day, then multiply it by 80, and that's about the figure. I had no idea that camels, elephants, mules, oxen, pigeons, dogs and cats perished in their thousands, often from starvation, cold and exhaustion, or because the soldiers had absolutely no idea how to look after them.

This is not a pretty story – it has been written with tears, not ink. Locked away in my study day after day, the material was so harrowing, I was in despair that I would ever be able to finish the book. But gradually I succumbed to the fascination of the subject. For with military history you put your finger on the pulse of all history, and so open the jewel box of the past. Gradually I realised too that it was not just a dry-as-dust subject dealing with tactics and strategies, but a story as full as any great novel of hatreds, petty jealousies, bumbling incompetence, burning ambition, and above all love. For where animals are concerned there is always love. One thinks of the Indian muleteers paid £1.20 a month, who refused ever to go on leave because they couldn't bear to be parted from their beloved mules, or the German horse who stopped in the middle of a cavalry charge, and trotted back to comfort his dying master until a shell killed them both, or of the bedraggled mongrel in the trenches running desperately from soldier to soldier, gradually coming to the end of his little strength as he frantically searched for his missing master.

Fortunately too where animals are concerned, comedy is never far away either. As each chapter was started, and I became acquainted with each new animal, I would wander downstairs announcing: 'I must have a mule, they're so wonderful,' or 'Do you think we could find room in the paddock for a baby camel, or even an ox, they're so terribly brave?'

As I type this introduction, my two dogs sleep sleekly beneath the table, and a large black cat purrs in my In tray. Across the valley, cows and sheep graze safely in the fields, and among them two beautiful slightly muddy grey horses, suddenly kick up their heels and, full of the joy of life, break into a gallop, manes and tails streaming. This is how animals should live, not dragged, terrified and suffering, into our human conflicts.

I am well aware that many many aspects of animals in war have been covered sketchily, some not at all, but if this book should make a few people aware of the immeasurable debt we owe to the animal kingdom for our freedom today, I shall be very happy.

Gloucestershire, 1983

My Kingdom for a Horse

'Do you know what they fought about?' I asked.

'No,' he said, 'that is more than a horse can understand; but the enemy must have been awfully wicked if it was right to go all that way over the sea on purpose to kill them.'

Anna Sewell: BLACK BEAUTY

On the morning of Tuesday 20 July 1982, a new guard formed by the Blues and Royals Mounted Squadron rode out from Hyde Park Barracks to take over as the Guards at Whitehall. Well aware that they were the loveliest sight in London, they rode with pride, and the usual crowd gathered along the pavement to marvel and applaud. Just as they were approaching Hyde Park Corner, a nail bomb hidden in a nearby car was detonated, killing four members of the guard. What sent shock waves of horror and outrage through the world, however, was that seven of the beautiful, glossy black horses which carried the soldiers were also killed and three severely wounded. Sefton, at nineteen the oldest, was the most badly injured. His jugular vein was completely severed and a six inch nail had pierced straight through his bridle into his head. After twenty-eight pieces of shrapnel were removed from his body, he made a slow but complete recovery, and returned triumphantly to work in November, having become a national symbol of courage and stoicism.

While in no way belittling the horror and vicious cruelty of this tragedy, it was shortly afterwards that I started my research on the part horses have played in war, and gradually realised to my dismay that the Hyde Park bombings were the merest drop in the ocean compared with the sufferings and terrors horses have endured in battle over the years. At least the dreadfully maimed horses in Hyde Park were immediately put out of their misery, or nursed back to health by devoted and highly skilled veterinary staff. They were not left to die slowly and in agony on the battlefield.

Of all the animals, the horse is probably the shyest, most highly strung and least aggressive. Yet for four thousand years he had been our most faithful ally in war. He has thundered unquestioningly into the mouth of the cannon. He has carried the military leaders and their vast armies to the far corners of the earth, allowing them to carve out their great empires. Yet despite the millions of words written to glorify the soldier's courage in war, little praise has been given to the horse that bore him. To single out a horse for praise seems to be as alien to most military commanders and historians as to suggest a tank or a helicopter fought with particular gallantry or stoicism.

Horses were first conscripted into armies sometime between 2000 and 1000 BC when a nomad tribe called the Hyksos invented a primitive form of chariot which could be drawn by a horse. With this weapon, they managed to overthrow the might of Egypt. A vast hurtling army of horses and chariots, raining down a torrent of sharp arrows, must have aroused the same kind of terror and panic we would feel today if a lot of Martians landed in spaceships. However, Egypt being a powerful nation soon drove out the Hyksos by inventing bigger and better chariots, this time drawn by two horses and carrying three men – one to drive and two to fire. By 1550 BC the chariot corps had become the elite of the Egyptian army.

It was Pharaoh's chariots who also drove the Israelis out of Egypt around the thirteenth century BC and instilled in them a marked antipathy to horses. Any Israeli capturing an enemy horse was ordered to hamstring him, which involved hacking through both tendons, leaving the wretched animal completely immobilised, crouching in dreadful pain under a burning sun until the vultures got him. This barbaric

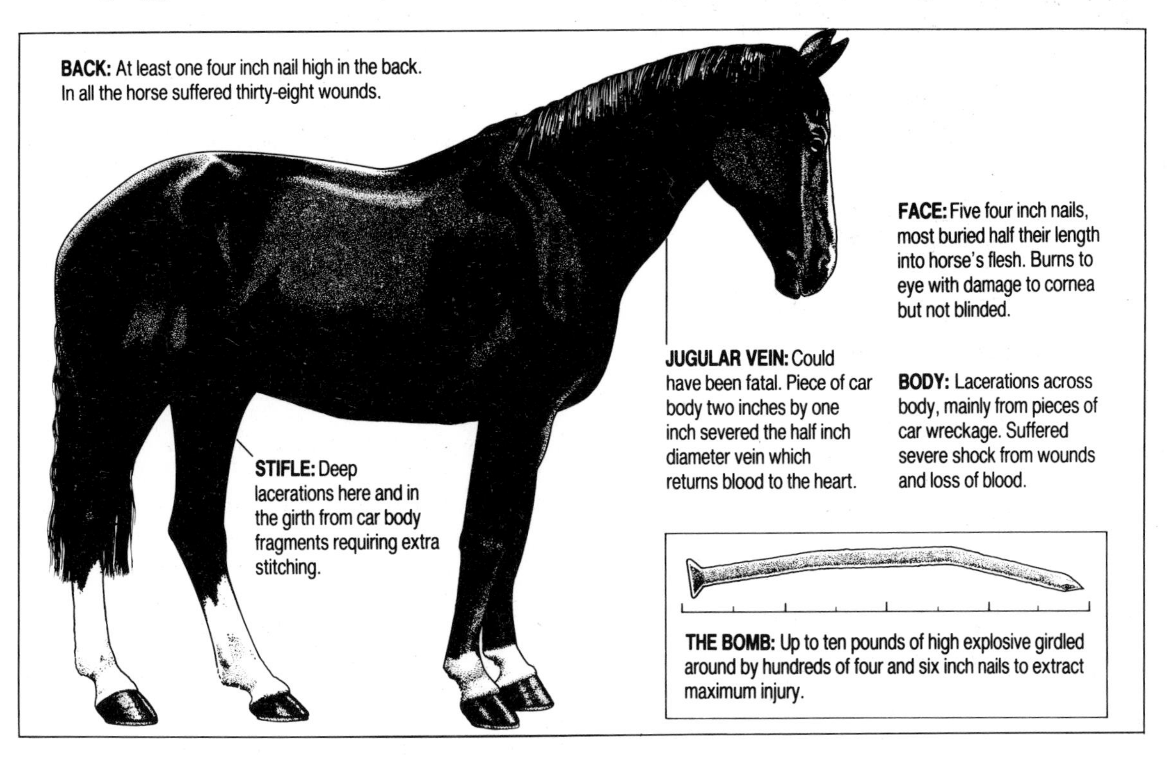

After 28 pieces of shrapnel were removed from his body, Sefton made a slow but complete recovery. The diagram gives details of his most serious injuries. (BY COURTESY OF *THE MAIL ON SUNDAY*)

and criminal practice continued for centuries. Rather as a soldier today would pull out the wiring from a vehicle, the Saracens used to hamstring their own horses during the Crusades rather than let them fall into the hands of the enemy.

The Greeks didn't use cavalry with any great efficiency until the fourth century BC, when Philip of Macedonia built up a well-drilled army which his son Alexander was later to exploit with such genius. Out of 40,000 men, 5,000 were cavalry. With this comparatively small force, Alexander was able to overthrow the might of Darius, King of Kings, who is estimated to have taken the field with a million foot soldiers, and 40,000 horsemen.

Alexander's revolutionary technique was to advance his infantry not in a straight line, but in the shape of a V pointing towards the enemy. This caused a dent in the opposing line, allowing his cavalry to sweep in on both flanks.

Alexander was exceptional among Greeks and among most early soldiers in that he was absolutely devoted to his horse Bucephalus. The name means 'Ox Head', the horse was so called because he had a particularly wide and handsome forehead. The legend goes that Philip, Alexander's father, had bought Bucephalus for a large sum, then found him vicious and unmanageable. The horse was about to be destroyed when Alexander, then aged twelve, asked if he might try and ride him. Despite the scoffing of his father, and no doubt the sniggering of the stable lads, he walked quietly up to Bucephalus, stroked him, swung his head towards the sun, and mounted him without difficulty. He was the only person to realise the horse was terrified by his own prancing shadow. The delighted Philip gave the horse to Alexander, who was also the only person Bucephalus ever allowed on his back.

Alexander rode Bucephalus through all his triumphant campaigns, but as the horse grew older, he used other horses for routine camp duties like inspecting and addressing the troops, and saved Bucephalus for the thick of the battle.

At the battle of Hydaspes in 326, when Alexander defeated the King of India, the gallant old warhorse who must have been at least thirty was wounded in the neck and side. Gushing blood, he carried the unscathed Alexander out of the fray, and only collapsed and died peacefully knowing his master was safe. Alexander was prostrate with grief. Bucephalus was buried with full military honours and a city was built over his grave.

The Romans were not wild about horses, preferring their splendidly drilled infantry; but they soon realised if they were going to carve out and hold an empire, they would need an efficient cavalry to stamp out border skirmishes and deal swift hammer blows at the crux of an infantry fight. During the fifth century AD, Roman supremacy was toppled by the Huns, terrifying hordes who thundered in on their small stocky ponies, burning, looting and terrorising all before them and darkening the sky with their arrows. The secret of the Huns' success was that, beside being inspired horsemen, they also introduced a brilliant new invention – the saddle. Made of wood and covered with hide, it kept the weight firmly off the horse's backbone by resting on his sides. Even more important, the saddle had two stirrups which enabled the rider to use all kinds of weapons, and to swing round in the saddle and fire arrows accurately at high speed. With the aid of stirrups, he could also deliver a blow using the combined weight of himself and his charging horses.

Had Attila triumphed at Châlons, Europe would have been totally under Asian rule for the first time in its history. After such a nasty fright, Europe learned

Alexander the Great – depicted as much younger than his alleged twelve years – about to tame the irascible Bucephalus.
MANSELL COLLECTION

fast, and soon all the armies were riding with saddles and stirrups. From the Bayeux Tapestry, we can see that William the Conqueror's cavalry rode with saddles, stirrups and spurs. The horses are still small, the riders' feet nearly touch the ground; and one winces at the thought of Harold's battleaxes hacking away at those delicate spindly legs and elegant heads.

From the tapestry it can also be seen that the knights are wearing both helmets and body stockings of chain mail. With the arrival of the Normans, we see the introduction of the fully armed knight into Britain.

The history of war has always been one of deterrent and counterdeterrent. The Norman knights on their nippy ponies and light armour could easily whisk out of range of Harold's battleaxes and bows and arrows. It therefore became necessary to produce a missile with a longer range, so the deadly crossbow was invented, and shortly afterwards the even more deadly longbow, which could shoot 250 yards (that's more than eleven cricket pitches) and bring down a horseman even before he started his charge.

The counterdeterrent was to resort to heavier armour for the rider, but then if his horse were hit, the rider was so hampered by his steel trappings that he couldn't run away, so the only answer was to arm the horse too. This meant that bigger and bigger horses were needed to carry all this weight, so we see the arrival of the heavy horse, or *destrier*, who was to dominate the battlefields of Europe until the invention of gunpowder ousted his supremacy.

The *destrier* was principally imported from the Low Countries and had hairy legs and huge quarters like our Shire horses today. By the twelfth century, he was carrying an armoured knight and armour on his own neck, head, forehead and hindquarters weighing up to thirty stone. It was no wonder that he could go no faster than a lumbering trot, and like armoured cars today, frequently got bogged down.

At the Battle of Bannockburn in 1314, for example, when Robert the Bruce defeated Edward II, the English *destriers* became completely bogged down in the marshy land and the potholes dug by the Scottish.

The Bayeux Tapestry, showing the cavalry of William the Conqueror. Note the use of stirrups, spurs, and body armour.
MANSELL COLLECTION

Edward III also imported a large number of horses from the Low Countries not only for stud purposes, but to continue the war against Scotland.

The cost of this influx of great horses so horrified the Archbishop of Canterbury in 1310 that he included the excessive expense of their upkeep among the worst abuses of the country. Each great horse cost 2s 7d a week to keep – a sum which would have fed at least four or five people.

It was impossible for the man in the street to afford, let alone keep or arm, one of these huge horses, so the animal became a status symbol of the very rich and grand, just like cars at the beginning of the twentieth century.

J.M. Brereton in his brilliant book, *The Horse in War*, writes, 'Drawn exclusively from the nobility and "county" families, the elite ranks of the mounted knights were everywhere regarded as the flower of military might . . . on the battlefield the knight and his horse reigned supreme, they had become the raison d'être of the armies, and the humble serfs and peasants of the infantry were regarded as little more than a nuisance.'

Occasionally the infantry were allowed to start the battle, but if their skirmishing went on too long, the mounted knights got fed up with waiting, and charged into and over their wretched followers.

It was this superiority of the mediaeval knight that somehow instilled into the cavalry the idea that they would always be smarter than any other section of the army. This attitude was summed up several hundred years later by the young officer who when asked in a *Punch* joke to define the role of the cavalry in war, replied: 'I suppose to give tone to what would otherwise be a mere vulgar brawl.'

With the arrival of gunpowder, the heavy horse's reign was ended. At the Battle of Crécy in 1346, 8,500 English infantry routed a French army of 50,000. Armed with long bows and three very primitive cannon, the English also had the advantage of having their backs to a low slanting evening sun. Standing their ground, as the French *destriers* and their riders clanked forward like Metal Mickies, the English let loose a volley of arrows and gunpowder, bringing the horses crashing to the ground. Even if they weren't hurt, it was difficult for them to get up in all that armour, and many were trampled underfoot as the French cavalry put in fifteen gallant but equally ineffectual charges. The French lost 11,500 men, the English a mere 200.

'It is best', as J.M. Brereton points out, 'not to contemplate the image of the stricken *destrier*, pierced with a dozen barbed shafts, each convulsive struggle forcing them deeper and deeper and twisting them in his entrails.'

Nevertheless, at the Battle of Mancura during the Crusades, one horse, obviously an early Sefton, staggered out of the fray like a maddened porcupine with fifteen arrows sticking out of him, and survived.

Now that gunpowder had arrived, it was not long before the cavalry, determined not to be upstaged, picked up their muskets too. Gustavus of Sweden ordered his mounted men to ride at the enemy, fire a single shot, and then set to with the sword. At Edgehill, in 1642, Prince Rupert banned muskets altogether, insisting that his men galloped home with the sword alone.

Rupert is probably one of the most glamorous figures in English history, a handsome foreign prince and a brilliant commander who fought for the Royalist cause out of sheer altruism. It is fitting that his concept of the charge, tearing across country like a hunt in full cry, and brandishing a sword instead of a whip, should become the romantic dream of every cavalryman, whenever he entered the fray.

Marlborough like Prince Rupert preferred his cavalry to use the sword not the pistol, and to advance at a steady trot. He was also a stickler for neatness, deploring long messy tails, and insisting the horses had their tails docked ludicrously short like a boxer dog's stump, leaving them with no protection against flies. Even more barbaric was the practice of having their ears cut short, on the premise that the wretched animals might go beserk if the offending protruberances were suddenly lopped off by some complicated sword flourish in war.

In the eighteenth century Frederick the Great probably created one of the most efficient armies of

October 1813: Wellington's forces crossing the Bidassoa River into French territory. From the painting by J.P. Beadle. MANSELL COLLECTION

modern times. He found his cavalry in a chaotic state, with the men riding sloppily and the horses fat as elephants. With extensive drilling he soon had horses and riders welded together like centaurs. Frederick also had the vision to realise that as gunpowder grew more efficient, the cavalry would become more vulnerable without any artillery backup. He therefore introduced batteries of light six-pounder guns, balanced on gun carriages, and drawn by six galloping horses, which were able to keep up with the cavalry wherever they went. Once again Europe was not slow to follow suit, soon every cavalry had its team of galloping gunners. The British model, founded in 1793, became the Royal Horse Artillery.

Napoleon was another great military leader who found his cavalry in a chaotic state and took immediate steps to remedy the situation. Although he was determined to improve the quality of the horses, he had absolutely no feelings about the animals themselves, and made it very clear that he didn't wish horses to be spared if they could catch men.

And they were not spared. In the retreat from Moscow in 1812, Murat lost a horrifying 30,000 horses, who either starved or froze to death. Little better was the fate of the British horses in the Peninsular War. On the retreat to Corunna, horses, with riders in the saddle, were discovered frozen stiff like equestrian statues.

Then came the 'most unkindest cut of all'. Having survived all the horrors, any of the horses that staggered into Corunna had to be shot by the soldiers, as there was no room on the boats, and they mustn't fall into enemy hands.

According to J.M. Brereton, 'a horrifying carnage ensued, there was no time for humane consideration, only a mass slaughter with troopers unused to pistols, firing into the demented herds. Maimed and mangled horses struggled or lay still, on the quayside . . . or panic-stricken, galloped over the edge of the quay and were left to drown . . . when ammunition ran short, the troops were ordered to use the sword and even worse butchery ensued.'

One poignant aspect of the tragedy, and one that crops up frequently in the next hundred and fifty years of war, was that only the soldiers' horses were slaughtered. Room was found on the boats for nearly all the officers' chargers – as usual there was one law for the rich and privileged.

Not that the soldiers appeared to be particularly attached to their horses. Captain A.C. Mercer of G. Troop R.H.A. commented acidly in his journal of the Waterloo campaign, that the only way to make the men pay some attention to their horses was to make them walk and carry their kit should their horses fall sick or die.

Waterloo had its own share of terrible casualties. In twelve successive charges, the French light cavalry under Marshal Ney crashed against the immovable squares of Wellington's redcoats. Each charge was hampered by dead and dying horses underfoot, and grass made slippery by spilt blood. Marshal Ney had three horses shot from under him.

Two extracts from Captain Mercer's diary, however, illustrate the full horror of the battle. At the height of the fighting, he noticed some soldiers hastily unharnessing a battery horse, and shooing it away. A few minutes later he was amazed to see the horse desperately trying to join another team, looking down he was sickened to see that the lower half of the animal's head had been shot away. 'Still he lived, and seemed conscious of all around whilst his full clear eyes seemed to implore us not to chase him away from his companions.'

Fortunately, Mercer ordered a farrier to destroy the horse. Later, his own brave troop of horses were badly shot to pieces and those left alive suffered a dreadful night on the battlefield. 'Some lay on the ground with entrails hanging out, one poor animal excited painful interest, he had lost, I believe, both his hind legs, and there he sat the night long on his tail, looking about as if in expectation of coming aid, sending forth from time to time long and protracted melancholy neighing.'

Anyone who has watched the Grand National will appreciate the herd instinct of the horse. In battle it was the same; a horse would be so terrified that he would keep going however badly he was injured, racing along, being careful not to tread on dead or wounded bodies, until he came to three or four other riderless horses, and would fall in with them keeping together for mutual protection. This herd instinct was also tragically illustrated at the Charge of the Light Brigade during the Crimean War when horribly mutilated horses instinctively followed the nearest rider and had to be beaten off with the sword. Theirs was not even the ability to reason why.

And if the carnage effected on the Light Brigade wasn't enough, the Crimean winter did the rest. It didn't appear to occur to the authorities that horses tied up in the freezing cold would never survive without food or clothing. There was no hay and no rugs, and the demented horses started eating each others' manes and tails.

A report from the *Illustrated London News* of February 3 1855 says it all:

> Once . . . he had been a handsome charger, but now he was the veriest caricature, a skeleton covered by an old hide, no mane, no tail; deep set ghastly glaring eyes, and lips sunk away from the long hungry teeth. You could not tell the colour, his hair was covered with a thick coat of mud, which fitted like a slush covered leather jerkin, there he stood shivering in the sun up to his knees in mire, tied to what had

once been a shrub, but was now no more than a bundle of withered leafless stalks.

Fortunately rumblings of disapproval were beginning to be heard. The late nineteenth century saw the growth of that splendidly vigilant organisation the R.S.P.C.A. At the beginning of the Franco-Prussian War, they wrote to both combatants pleading that a corps of official slaughterers might be employed to put wounded horses out of their misery. With massive contempt the Germans appointed one man. He was not much use. The R.S.P.C.A. in their magazine *Animal World* gave an infinitely pathetic account of the aftermath of the Battle of Vionville, when hundreds of horses lay wounded on the battlefield. Evidently, when the bugler for the first regiment of German Dragoon Guards sounded the evening call, 602 wounded horses answered the summons. Shuffling, terribly lame, some scarcely able to crawl, the noble creatures staggered back to the lines.

'One can guess,' wrote *Animal World*, 'the feelings of the German Dragoons when they beheld this touching scene, and many a hand brushed away a tear.'

Compassion also shone through the carnage after the Battle of Omdurman in 1898, when troopers of the 21st Lancers gave their heavily wounded horses, those that could hobble down the river, a long, last drink before shooting them.

Prince Albert and his own? An example of the glamour of the 'Arme Blanche' as typified by the Prince Consort in the Uniform of the 11th Hussars. LC

THE CORNER

The oxen team is much in evidence in the march past of the victorious British forces in Pretoria in June 1900. IWM

In fact as Lord Anglesey points out in Volume III of his *History of the British Cavalry*, as the nineteenth century drew to a close, people were starting to be more professional about the horse. Remounts are spare army horses. In 1887 an Army Remount Centre was founded which consisted of a pool of horses on which each regiment could draw, if it fell below its allotted equine quota. Thus 'no longer would the buying of horses be subjected to the whims of individual commanding officers, and the wiles of dealers'. Remounts, it was further ruled in 1898, must be at least fifteen hands high, and five years old.

In 1888 under the National Defence Act a system of organisation was started, giving the Government powers to requisition horses in times of national danger. Livery stable keepers, bus and railway companies were all asked to register a percentage of their livestock and by 1897 some 14,500 horses were on the books.

Meanwhile across the Atlantic, the American Civil War of 1861–5 had come and gone, which was not only the greatest clash since the Napoleonic Wars, but also introduced a revolution in cavalry tactics. Charging against the newer, more powerful and accurate guns, generals on both sides found they were losing too many horses.

The new technique was therefore to gallop within gunfire range of the enemy, leap off your horse, leaving him in charge of a soldier, then pound away at the enemy until your ammunition ran out, then if you were still alive, you jumped on to your rested horse, and galloped away to safety.

Unfortunately, the British, wrapped in their usual isolation, took absolutely no notice of these new tactics and continued to dream of the knee-to-knee cavalry charge.

It was hardly surprising that when they arrived in South Africa in 1899, supremely confident of crushing the Boers in a few weeks, they were dismayed to find themselves outshot and outridden by gangs of 'Bible thumping farmers mounted on scruffy little ponies'. These tough Boer ponies in fact could live off the land and keep going for days, while their masters as well as being first class shots, knew the country backwards,

Watering the horses: a Boer War situation which was not always as simple as it is depicted. IWM

and kept well out of the way so the British cavalry had no one to charge.

Most important of all, having learnt the lesson of the American Civil War, the Boers dismounted when they reached the enemy, and used their guns. Nor did they need any extra hands to hold their ponies, who were trained to stand still the moment their reins were thrown over their heads. By comparison, the British horses, after a dreadful sea trip round the Cape, were given no time to rest and get used to the climate. Nor had the British learnt from the Crimean War that the hunter, the mainstay of their cavalry, though brilliant at keeping going at speed across country, cannot thrive on short rations and violent shifts in temperature. The only British horses who turned out to be tough enough to stand up to the conditions were those sent out by the London Bus Company.

The other equine success story of the Boer War was the Australian Waler. The product of thoroughbred stallions bought cheap from England and mated with local mares, the Walers were light but extremely tough, and used to carrying their masters all day on

Boot, saddle, to horse. . . British yeomanry in the Boer War. IWM

the sheep farm. They had no difficulty coping with the long treks, nor the shortage of hay and oats, or the shifting climate.

The Australian bushmen who accompanied them brought their usual cheerful iconoclasm to the battle. A troop under Herbert Plumer, who was later to become a distinguished general, was encamped with some Dragoon Guards. Soon the Dragoon's fine chargers began to vanish from the horse lines, with the scruffy Walers taking their place. The incensed Dragoons found it hard to identify their horses (give an Australian half an hour with a horse, and tails are changed, manes hogged, and brands and marks disappear like magic) and complained bitterly to Plumer. He was totally unsympathetic, telling them they could learn a few lessons in tactics and toughness from the bushmen. He was less amused however when someone stole his fine grey charger and dyed it with Condy's fluid. The General with his eyeglass picked out the horse from the Australian lines, and the guilty bushman was made to walk for a day beside his mounted comrades.

Parley between surrendering Boers and 1st East Lancs, 1900. IWM

In fact the Dragoons' fine horses were soon breaking down like the other British horses from exhaustion, mange, strangles, influenza, and sore backs. Even worse, at Ladysmith and Mafeking, the cavalry were forced to shoot their horses to feed the starving garrisons, and fight as infantry. Every bit of the horse was used. Tails and manes stuffed mattresses, bones were boiled to make soup, flesh was minced and stuffed into intestines to make sausages.

Britain won the war in the end by sheer weight of numbers, but the horse casualties were a disgrace. Out of the 520,000 remounts supplied, an utterly appalling 326,073 horses died – most of them from disease and exhaustion rather than enemy fire. Never before in the history of any war had there been such a dreadful sacrifice of animal life and public money. And because there was no veterinary corps to destroy the sick and wounded horses or supervise their return, they brought home diseases, which weren't stamped out for years.

At the beginning of the Boer War, the R.S.P.C.A. had been on the warpath again. After much fuss they were assured by the British authorities that although they didn't feel an official corps to put horses down was necessary, directions had been given to all the troopers to end mercifully the lives of all severely wounded animals. This was plainly rubbish. A trooper can't shoot a horse, if he's running for his life, or severely wounded. According to an R.S.P.C.A. pamphlet issued after the war, one of the most painful recollections of the soldiers in the Boer War was the heavy moaning of the injured horses, and their sorrow at having to abandon these doomed creatures in their hour of misery.

Public feeling was outraged. In 1902 a parliamentary committee was set up. As a result, the Army Veterinary Corps was founded in 1903, with Major-General Frank Smith, a man of great vision and compassion, appointed Director-General. He vowed that in future the corps would keep animal suffering and wastage to a minimum. How triumphantly it was to achieve this aim despite appalling obstacles and setbacks will be seen in the next chapter.

Goodbye, Old Man

'Most obediently and often most painfully they died – faithful unto death.'

INSCRIPTION ON THE WAR MEMORIAL TO HORSES AT ST JUDE ON THE HILL, HAMPSTEAD.

With the coming of the motor car and the bicycle, the horse population in England dwindled to such an extent that when war was declared in 1914, there was a huge dearth of suitable animals. Tillings, the London Bus Company, for example, who were already busy converting to horseless carriages, made a fortune selling a great many of their remaining horses to the army. Later farmers in America, Argentina, Canada and Australia grew rich exporting horses to the allies. But one of the cruellest ordeals for private owners in this country was when their family pets were called up. It seemed a kind of betrayal; you couldn't explain to a horse why he was being sent away. John Galsworthy expressed unashamed relief when his chestnut mare was rejected as unfit, and there exists a touching

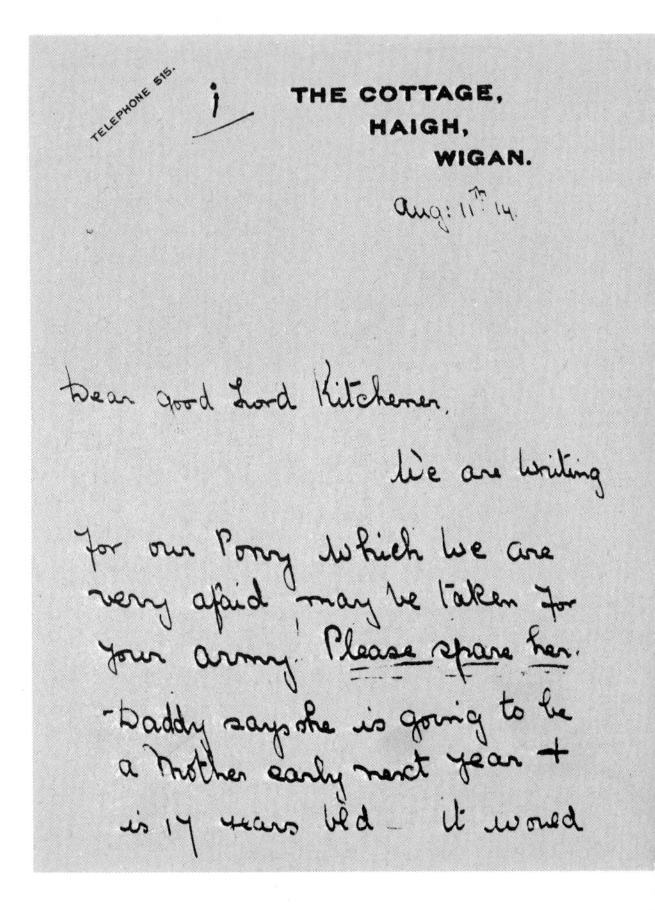

TELEPHONE 515.

THE COTTAGE,
HAIGH,
WIGAN.

Aug: 11th 14.

Dear good Lord Kitchener,

We are writing for our Pony which we are very afaid may be taken for your army. Please spare her. Daddy says she is going to be a Mother early next year & is 17 years old. It would correspondence between some children and the War Office. Poppy, Lionel, and Freda Hewlett wrote on 11 August 1914:

Dear Lord Kitchener,
We are writing for our pony, which we are very afraid may be taken for your army. Please spare her. Daddy says she is going to be a mother early next year, and is 17 years old. It would break our hearts to let her go. We have given 2 others and 3 of our family are now fighting for you in the Navy. Mother and all will do anything for you but do please let us keep old Betty, and send official word *quickly* before anyone comes.

Your troubled little Britishers
P.L. and Freda Hewlett

Happily Lord Kitchener's heart was touched. His private secretary wrote back by return of post, enclosing a note from the Colonel in charge of remounts, 'F.M. Lord Kitchener has decided that no horses under 15 hands shall be requisitioned from the British family: P.L. and Freda Hewlett.'

The overjoyed Hewletts replied:

To our good Lord Kitchener, You are indeed kind to allow us to keep our dear old Betty. We met every post and hardly dared to hope *you*, who have so much to do, had had time to read our request, so little to you – so much to us. . . . Always and ever your grateful British servants.

Other owners were not so lucky, but shored themselves up with the belief that war would be over

13th August 1914.

Dear Miss Freda Hewlett,

Lord Kitchener asks me to say in reply to your letter of the 11th August, that if you will show the enclosed note to anyone who comes to ask about your pony, he thinks it will be left to you quite safely.

Yours very truly,

H J Creedy

Private Secretary.

Miss Freda Hewlett,
The Cottage,
Haigh, Wigan.

War Office,
Whitehall,
S.W.

F.M. Lord Kitchener has directed that no horses under 15 hands shall be requisitioned belonging to the British family P. L & Freda Hewlett soon – as is shown by this poem from an R.S.P.C.A. anthology, sold to raise money for wounded horses:

We didn't know much about it.
We thought they'd all come back
But off they all were taken
White and Brown and Black;
Cart and Cab and Carriage,
Wagon and Break and Dray,
Went out at the call of duty.
And we watched them go away.
All of their grieving owners
Led them along the lane
Down the hill to the station.
And saw them off by train.
They must be back by Xmas,
And won't we give them a feed.

But alas they were not back for many Christmases if at all, because no one had anticipated the colossal scale on which horses would be needed. Within a few months of war breaking out, the two opposing sides were locked in a stalemate of trench warfare. This meant endless static lines of guns pounding the hell out of each other, pouring forth an endless stream of shells which broke up the ground, destroyed the drainage systems, and transformed the surrounding countryside for miles around into a treacherous sea of mud.

These pounding lines of guns had to be continually fed as did the men in the trenches, but the ground was in such a frightful state that lorries and trucks were bogged down in a trice. Only teams of horses or mules could get the ammunition and supplies up to the front, and if the line advanced or retreated a mile or two, only they could lug the guns into their new position.

The land they had to cross was a vast honeycomb of huge craters filled with thick fetid mud. These craters often interlocked and were so deep, that if a shell landed in one, it was several seconds before it hit the bottom, detonated and spewed forth a fountain of burning metal and poisonous slime. Over this fearful network of death traps, the wretched teams floundered, desperately groping for firm ground, often at

Ammunition and limbers on the move towards Ypres, 25 September 1917. IWM

Many fell never to rise again. IWM

dead of night and through blizzard and storm. If a horse shied at a shell bursting overhead, or collapsed from exhaustion under his heavy load, or merely took a false step, he'd be into a shell hole in a second, slithering down the greasy sides. His driver would make heroic attempts to rescue him, but there was always a risk that the rest of the team might be sucked under too, so a bullet through the head was usually the most the horse could hope for.

Mr Sydney Smith, now aged eighty, remembers being a private on the Somme:

'Nothing as far as the eye could see except waves rippling the mud as the wind blew, I had the terrible experience to witness three horses and six men disappear completely under the mud. It was a sight that will live for ever in my memory, the cries of the trapped soldiers were indescribable, as they struggled to free themselves. The last horse went to a muddy grave, keeping his nostrils above the slush until the last second. A spurt of mud told me it was all over.'

Having struggled up to the line, the teams had then to stagger back for another load: men and horses, plastered from head to foot with yellow stinking mud, often bearing hideous wounds, and using the carcasses of dead animals and humans as stepping stones under a bombardment that could even be heard across the channel in the Kentish ports.

The chief enemy, in fact, was never the Germans with their shot and shell, but the terrible weather and

A view of the shell-cratered ground over which troops and animals of both sides had to cross. Passchendaele, October, 1917. A typical shell hole is in the foreground. IWM appalling conditions. Out of 256,000 horses lost by the British on the Western Front, only 58,000 or fewer than a quarter were destroyed by enemy fire. Worst of all, during the first winter of the war, was the risk of death from overexposure. The retreat from Mons had put all plans for stabling and hospital accommodation askew and the wretched horses had to be picketed out in the open. An Exmoor or New Forest pony can survive outside in winter because he keeps moving and grows a thick shaggy coat for protection. The delicate army horses, used to living in stables, were not only tied up, but also, because the army believed long coats led to mange, clipped out as well. Imagine these hapless beasts, wind and driving rain needling their nonexistent coats, standing hock deep in mud. In vain a horse picked one foot out of the mud: the other would sink in just as far, to be pulled out in its turn, a moment later. On this treadmill what rest could he get?

Matters would have been better if he had been given warm food and plenty of it, but in that first winter, and often later in the war, fodder was desperately short, with no overhead hay nets; so whatever there was, was trampled into the mud or blew away. Often the poor beasts were so hungry they ate their own sodden rugs, choking to death over the buckles. Sometimes they were so desperate that they tore the epaulettes off the men's shoulders.

Many of the horses suffered from harness sores and girth galls, and because there was no dubbin or saddle soap, the men improvised with bacon fat or bully beef. Later when there was time to put up makeshift stables, they were sometimes built over time bombs laid by the enemy. These exploded a foot off the ground with splinters striking the feet and belly of the horse, and sometimes completely disembowelling him.

There were also two kinds of gas to contend with. Mustard gas arrived in shells from a gun, the least touch on the skin leading to blisters, which when severe led to terrible multi-coloured burns. It was also a serious eye irritant. If warning were given in time, the horses were cut loose and driven from the area, but the gas evaporated slowly, and even after two days, horses could be affected by eating poisoned grass. Chlorine gas was sent forward in clouds or sometimes shells, and did appalling damage to the respiratory system. Generally, horses weren't as badly affected by gas as the soldiers. Between 1916 and 1918 there were only 2,220 horse casualties from gas, and only 211 died. Prevention tended to be even more unpleasant than the actual disease. When gas first appeared, gauze nose plugs were forced up each of the horse's nostrils, and held in place by three safety pins through the actual nose like some gruesome early punk. The inhumanity of this device fortunately prevented it from being widely used. Nor was the gas mask that appeared later much more successful. Made of flannel, the horses mistook it for a nosebag, and rootled irritably around looking for oats – with the result that the gas mask lasted about three minutes.

Many horses seemed to know the difference between enemy and friendly planes. One black polo pony used suddenly to stop, toss her head, and begin to stamp and neigh – sure enough five minutes later, enemy planes would appear overhead. When our planes flew past, she ignored them and carried on feeding.

The better bred the horses, the more they tended to suffer from shellshock. Horses would seem to give under their riders, break out in a fearful sweat, and refuse to go on. They would also shy away or bolt past any exposed spot or dangerous crossroads, where perhaps three months before they had stopped a bit of shrapnel. One mare became so badly affected, that when the French sappers blew up a bridge over the Aisne, she went beserk and rushed round kicking several men, and had to be shot. Others grew crafty, and when they saw their drivers taking cover, would duck their heads, drop on their knees or even lie down.

One of the redeeming features of this terrible war was the devotion that grew between the soldier and his horse. As J.M. Brereton points out in *The Horse in War*: 'On campaign, riding and tending the same horse for months on end, sleeping in the open only a few yards behind the picket lines at night, and suffering the same privations, the soldier came to regard his horse as almost an extension of his own being.'

Brereton goes on to deny that the famous painting

Gas masks or nosebags? A German transport driver and his team. IWM

by Matania, *Goodbye Old Man* (p. 41), which shows a soldier kneeling to hold his dying horse's head, is over-sentimental. Perhaps it was based on an act of heroism which occurred during one of the most desperate attacks along the Aisne. A boy from the Gloucestershire Regiment noticed that a horse, struck by a shell, was in great pain and neighing piteously for water. Although the Germans were closing in the boy hunted round for and found some water. When the position was retaken next day, the horse and the Gloucestershire lad were found together, dead.

There is no doubt either that the horses got just as fond of their owners. A Royal Field Artillery driver, a Welshman, had been with the same team for three years. He tells a poignant story that during the retreat from Mons, a shell crashed into the middle of his section. As the gun was wrecked, he was immediately ordered on to another. As he mounted his new horse, and continued the retreat, he saw his old horses flailing on the ground, and was relieved when a French chasseur rushed up and cut the traces. Seeing their old driver ahead, they followed him for four days.

We stopped for hardly five minutes, and I couldn't get back to them. They were in the line watching me so anxiously and sorrowfully as to make me feel guilty. Whenever the word Halt ran down the column I held up my hand, and they saw it every time and stopped. I don't know if they got anything to eat or dropped from sheer exhaustion. One morning when the retreat was all over, I missed them. That's the sort of thing that hurts a soldier in war.

Another redeeming feature about World War I was that it was the first war which had the advantage of a properly trained veterinary service. In 1913, sanction had been given for a mobile veterinary section to be attached to every cavalry and infantry brigade to pick up sick and lame animals shed during the fighting. Each brigade also had a veterinary officer who kept well forward where his services were most urgently needed, dressing wounds, treating minor ailments, and sending more serious cases back to field or base hospitals. Horses who couldn't walk went by ambulance. Each horse evacuated to hospital was issued with a special roll of paper, giving his serial number, unit, and the reason he'd been sent off sick, together with a

A fine sense of priorities: the Albert-Amiens road, August 1916. IWM

Wounded horses being led onto barges for transport to a veterinary hospital. Canal de l'Aa, St. Omer, 9 June 1918. IWM descriptive label: green for surgical, white for medical cases and red for mange or other contagious diseases.

During the four and a half years of war, 2,562,549 horses and mules were admitted to veterinary hospitals in France. It was a staggering achievement that nearly two million were cured and returned to duty. It must have been heartbreaking for the men working in the hospitals, nursing desperately wounded horses back to health and confidence, only to send them back to the horrors of the front line. But there was a war to be won, and horses had to be cured to keep the army going. The value of the Army Veterinary Corps can perhaps best be appreciated when one realises that the Germans lost four horses to our one, simply through lack of care. They didn't bother to shoot or cure their wounded horses, they merely dumped them – often to the advantage of the British. One German mare was picked up by a young veterinary corps assistant with three bullets deep in her shoulder. Against his supervisor's advice, he operated, removed the bullets, and in a short time, the horse was as right as rain.

There were, however, moments when members of the Corps were slightly less splendid, as can be seen from the hilarious diary of a veterinary officer, who joined up in 1916, and was attached to the Brigade. Sadly, he was obviously too fraught to make more than a few entries:

> '1916 March: No horse. Borrowed one, ran away with me. March 24: First night of shelling, horses picketed out in very swampy field. Rode big bay mare, ran away with me, terrified of running into motor lorry, steered for the ditch, she stopped, I came off.'

Sometimes, too, the soldiers felt the veterinary officers made very wrong decisions. In *Animal World*, the R.S.P.C.A. printed a letter from some Royal Field Artillery officers describing their departure to France in 1916:

> At Southampton, we lost our dear Sailor, our prize horse, who caught the veterinary officer's eye, who insisted he was too old, too thin and unfit for service. He didn't know. He only judged by appearances. Sailor wasn't worth much too look at, but was worth six horses in the battery. If a gun team jibbed, we hitched old Sailor and he pulled through the whole show. If a vehicle got stuck in a ditch, or was too heavy to start, old Sailor moved it. He would work for 24 hours without winking, and he was as quiet as a lamb and as clever as a thoroughbred, but he looked like nothing on earth, so we lost him, and the whole battery kissed him goodbye and the drivers and gunners, who fed him, nearly cried.

As the war dragged on, more and more men were called up who knew absolutely nothing about horses. The Director of Veterinary Services in France tried to remedy this situation by instituting ten-day courses on horse management, with 300 N.C.O.s and 550 officers taking the course each month. Sometimes the lecturers must have had to be very patient. One young infantry officer in charge of 50 horses complained to the Assistant Director of Veterinary Services about the poor quality of the oats.

'Well sir,' he explained petulantly, 'They're so small they get stuck in the horse's teeth.'

'That's tough,' replied the A.D.V.S. 'You'd better indent for a supply of toothpicks.'

Horses ready for discharge from No. 5 Veterinary Hospital, Abbeville, 3 March 1916. IWM

But if the A.V.C. had difficulties in France, they were nothing compared with their ordeals in other theatres of war. In Gallipoli, for example, the horse lines were on the beaches well within range of the enemy, and the horses were subjected to shell and machine gun fire all night and whenever they went to water. Ten days after the landings, the beaches were shelled every afternoon and evening. For three days, all the veterinary officers could do was to hide in dugouts, and run out during intervals in shelling to shoot the seriously wounded horses.

They also had a terrible time trying to operate on animals. On several occasions a horse had been laid flat and anaesthetised, and had to be hurriedly got up in the middle of surgery, so that the men could take cover. Dust storms frequently made dressing wounds intolerable, and flies were everywhere, alleged to be even more trouble to the mules than was the enemy fire.

In July, August and September, the heat was so terrible, and fever and dysentery were so rampant among both officers and men, that hardly anyone was on his feet to look after the horses. On a more macabre note, there were even greater problems in burying all the dead horses. Exhausted troops had to dig huge graves in sandy places, and as the sand was thrown out, it fell back in again at the sides. Matters reached a level of black comedy, when an attempt was made to float carcasses out to sea. They wouldn't sink, and the hooves, protruding out of the water, were on more than one occasion mistaken for the periscopes of hostile submarines.

Even more hideous conditions prevailed in South Africa, where in 1915 there was a complete breakdown of the railways, and therefore of forage supplies. The veterinary and remount departments had 60,000 debilitated animals on their hands in various camps in the desert, and nothing to feed them on. The animals were too weak to trek to places on the coast, where thousands of tons of forage were waiting. Whenever attempts were made, the route was merely strewn with corpses. For four appalling months, from July to October, veterinary officers sent increasingly desperate telegrams every day, and impotently watched the maddened horses slowly dying of starvation and so desperate that many of them ate their own droppings. By the time supplies finally began to filter through in November, many thousands of horses had died or been destroyed.

'The only qualification you needed,' said one veterinary officer bitterly, 'was to be a good shot.'

But there is no doubt of the invaluable part played by the A.V.C. in winning the war. According to Haig, if Germany's equine force had been as strong they could have broken the British and French armies. For its efforts 'in mitigating animal suffering, in increasing the mobility of the mounted units, and for reducing animal wastage', the Army Veterinary Corps richly deserved to have the prefix Royal added to its name in 1918.

The other great band of fairy godmothers to the war horse was once again the R.S.P.C.A. Immediately war was declared in 1914, the Society offered its services to the War Office in any way that might be useful. The offer was abruptly turned down on the grounds that the organisation of the A.V.C. was so complete that no outside assistance was needed.

Under the circumstances, the only thing the R.S.P.C.A. could do was turn the other cheek, and encourage as many as possible of its inspectors to join the A.V.C. Ninety did so. The Society also unofficially supplied horse ambulances to various units training at home who asked for them, and many worthy ladies were kept busy knitting pads to prevent saddle sores.

It was soon found that the ninety R.S.P.C.A. inspectors who'd joined up were absolutely invaluable because of their discipline and knowledge of horses. After three months, the strain on the Army Veterinary Department was so great that on November 5, the Army Council climbed down and wrote that they would be very grateful if the R.S.P.C.A. would help them find more veterinary staff to join the Corps. There must have been many a quiet laugh at R.S.P.C.A. headquarters when the Council also humbly added that they would now be very happy if the R.S.P.C.A. set up an official fund to provide hospital equipment for the sick horses.

As a result, the Society collected and trained 200

This painting, captioned, 'Goodbye, Old Man', was used to raise funds for Animal Relief in the U.S.A. The original is by the well-known war artist Fortunino Matania. IWM

men, and its staff gave talks to hundreds of soldiers throughout the country on the care of horses. The R.S.P.C.A. Sick and Wounded Horse Fund was also officially opened. The first flag day was held in 1915. Those indomitable ladies set to with their collecting boxes, and by the end of the war had raised the colossal sum of more than £250,000.

The Society provided thirteen hospitals in France with room for 13,500 horses. The fund also paid for a complete convalescent depot, tented hospitals to accommodate a further 6,800 horses, 180 horse ambulance, 26 motor ambulances, costing more than £1000 each, and numerous horsey extras like rugs and corn crushers. Altogether it was a splendid achievement. The R.S.P.C.A. fund was particularly useful because it could supply the individual needs of the horses very quickly, whereas an application to the War Office was likely to get hopelessly enmeshed in red tape.

The R.S.P.C.A. was, in fact, the only society authorised by the War Office to raise money for the wounded horses. But mention must be made of the invaluable work of the Blue Cross, which also raised huge sums for the same purposes, and provided hospitals, ambulances, and supplies. By the end of the war, they had also built kennels for sick and wounded dogs, which were attached to all the base horse hospitals in France.

We must turn now to the fate of the cavalry horse. In the first few weeks of the war, colourful regiments of Hussars, Lancers and Dragoons rode out proudly on their splendid horses, fully confident that they were the élite of all the armies. But they soon found to their dismay that no one could charge across a honeycomb of shell holes, or through great entanglements of barbed wire.

On 24 August 1914 at Audregnies, 400 men from the 9th Lancers gallantly charged a solid mass of German infantry in the face of a torrent of shell and shot, and galloped on until they ran into two lines of barbed wire. Unable to pull up, men and horses went crashing over and 128 men, and many more fine horses, were killed. Some dashing charges and manoeuvres covered the advance and retreat from Mons, and there was the famous Canadian Cavalry Charge at Moreuil Woods on 30 March 1918, when three mounted troops of Lord Strathcona's Horse gallantly routed approximately 100 Germans armed with machine guns. According to Marshall Foch, 'The Canadian Cavalry by their magnificent attack first held the enemy in check then broke their forward march.' But the action was tragically costly in horses; of the 150 that went into the fray, only four survived. On the whole, though, when faced with machine guns and artillery fire, the cavalry were forced to dismount, and spend the rest of the war fighting on foot and hoping

for a break in the front lines, when they would be able to charge ahead on their horses once more.

On the Allied side, however, a large number of the military leaders were ex-cavalrymen who continued to be obsessed with the dream of the ultimate break-through, and who genuinely believed with General Haigh: 'that the bullet has no stopping power against the horse.' As a result, as J.M. Brereton points out in *The Horse In War*, 'Vast numbers of troop horses were kept in the field waiting the chance that never came. When the world's first tanks appeared in 1916, there were more than a million cavalry horses on all fronts.'

Battle of the Scarpe. British cavalry resting on the Arras-Cambrai road, April 1917. IWM

Convalescent horses under tents to shelter them from the middle-eastern sun. IWM

Yet if the Western Front offered little opportunity for dashing cavalry charges, General Allenby's triumphant campaign against the Turks in Egypt and Palestine proved that, given the right conditions, the horse, soldier, and shock tactics could still play a decisive role.

The campaign in Palestine in 1917–18 showed the cavalry at their superb best, handled as had seldom been their good fortune in earlier campaigns. The Desert Mounted Corps, as it was called, consisted of 20,000 men and horses drawn from Australia, New Zealand, the Indian Cavalry, and the British Yeomanry Regiments, and was the largest cavalry force to operate under one commander during the war. Their comrades in France must have looked on their achievements with ill-concealed envy.

But ironically while these comrades were drowning in the mud of the shell holes, the enemy in Palestine was lack of water. There were very few wells, and those there were, were very deep. If the Turks couldn't defend them, they blew them up, or destroyed the winding apparatus. This meant that each desperately parched horse had to be watered individually from a bucket laboriously lowered on the end of a rope made of telephone wires, or reins tied together.

Horses, as J.M. Brereton tells us, were usually watered at least four times a day. In Palestine they often went without water for sixty hours – pounding across burning sands under a white-hot sun, with each horse carrying at least twenty stone. The record was evidently achieved by the horses of the Worcestershire Yeomanry, who survived an incredible ninety hours without a drop of water, or any serious casualties – an act of endurance which can seldom have been surpassed.

Often at night, the horses were so tired that they refused to eat, and weary troops would knead dry grain into little balls moistened with a few last drops of water and feed the horses by hand. Another method of conserving the horse's strength was to carry a biscuit tin of water on the dashboard of every gun wagon; at hourly intervals, the men would wipe the mouths, eyes and nostrils of the horses with wet cloths. Invariably, too, the soldiers could be seen emptying the last drops out of their water bottles on to tin plates for their parched animals.

Frequently during the campaign, the horses went so long without water that their exhausted riders could barely control them as they stampeded the wells. It was inevitable that many of the battles with the Turks were fought for the crucial control of some watering place.

Take the Battle of Beersheba. On 31 October 1917, after a 24-hour march by the cavalry over unknown waterless country, it was essential to capture the Beersheba wells by nightfall, because many of the horses were so frantic with thirst they wouldn't survive. The Turkish defence of the village, however, was stubborn, and an hour before nightfall it was still holding out, with morale high. At sunset, armed only with bayonets, two regiments of Australian cavalry advanced in a long line at a gallop, half hidden in dust. Before them lay the enemy trenches, outlined like fireflies as the Turks rattled away with their guns. Suddenly as the Australians thundered on, the hailstorm of bullets ceased. The Turks were so amazed by this wild, totally unexpected charge that they had failed to lower their sights. There was the first trench – a shallow one – the horses leapt it easily. The next was deeper and wider, and filled with frightened upturned faces of the Turks, with their huddle of bayonets stretched up towards the horse's bellies. They were over. The Australians dismounted on the other side, and attacked with the bayonet; it was all over in ten minutes. Two thousand prisoners were taken, and 500 enemy were killed. Soon the pumps were pouring water into the long canvas troughs, and buckets and even hats were being filled for the thirst-crazed horses. The dazzling success of the charge and the capture of essential wells were the start of the defeat of the whole Turkish line.

In the assault on Jerusalem later that year conditions were very different. The soldiers had to clamber up the slippery rocky slopes of the Judean Hills on their hands and knees, with their plucky horses following them like well-trained dogs. The rain continued to bucket down; and soon in the lines the horses were standing hock deep in mud, whipped by icy winds, which must have been a frightful shock to their systems after the fearful heat of the summer. In January, they reached a camp on the shore of the Mediterranean. Lt.-Col. A.C.N. Olden, of the 10th Australian Light Horse, gives and enchanting picture of the horses arriving:

> They had been many times short of food, leg weary, and shin sore, they had carried their heavy load, first through the blinding red dust of Beersheba, then over the rubble and rocks and terraces of the Judean Hills, and finally through torrential rains and dust storms. They had not decently rested themselves for weeks, and what is much worse to a horse, they had not had a decent roll. Now they rolled and rolled and kept on rolling until it seemed they would never cease, and on that first night at Belah, after their evening feed, the stable pickets on duty reported 'every horse is down'.

The war itself was so terrible that any break in the hostilities seemed the more precious. Major Jack Fairfax-Blakeborough of the 9th Hussars wrote of the convalescent depot at Roclincourt: 'It was very hot in May 1917, there was little firing, and consequently little ammunition to take up to the line . . . I really did see horses improve here, and thoroughly enjoy life. We had a little steeplechase course put up, and jumping competitions . . . the summer was really lovely.'

In other parts of the war, one reads of officers sloping off for a little hunting or polo. Shoeing competitions were held for the farriers, and horse shows for the artillery with the guns and harnesses gleaming as brightly as the coats of the horses. In one fancy dress parade, a donkey appeared wearing khaki trousers. Even in the desert in Palestine in March 1917, they had a race meeting at Rafa. Events included the Promised Land Stakes, the Anzac Steeplechase, and even a Jerusalem Scurry for mules only. Trenches were filled in and jumps made of piled-up sandbags. Elyne Mitchell in her excellent book *Light Horse* points out that nearly every horse had carried his owner in the battle fought where he was now racing. The winner of the Sinai Grand National was one of the few survivors from a torpedoed horse transport who had since been wounded three times – thus showing the horse's amazing recuperative powers.

The Palestine Campaign was a particularly remarkable test of endurance because after 1917 no horse reinforcements were forthcoming. Eight thousand remounts were waiting in Australia, but there were no ships to carry them; everything that could sail was engaged in taking American troops to Europe. So casualties in Palestine were replaced by horses that had seen heavy service, often released from hospital before they had fully recovered. By September 1918, there was scarcely a fit horse behind the fighting troops. Finally on 31 October, Turkey surrendered.

Whether they were in France or Palestine, victory must have been as sweet to the exhausted horses as to the weary soldiers. According to Lt.-Col. D.S. Tamblyn, in an earlier work entitled *The Horse in War*, 'Horses and mules seemed to realise some great event had taken place, the feeling of nervousness was over, increased care suddenly bestowed on the horses gave them confidence.'

The entry into Mons was evidently a triumph. Troops on the march had flowers thrown in their path; the horses were patted by the people wherever they halted; and as the cavalry galloped through the streets liberating occupied villages, women tugged them off their horses, and flung their arms round the necks of both men and their mounts.

In Palestine after the fall of Damascus, the army of riders and horses who'd fought so bravely were surrounded by a cheering throng. Horses, used to anything, were happy to accept grapes, peaches and cream cakes, even having flowers fastened to their bridles.

Would that the story had ended with all these gallant creatures returning to England or their homelands, and leading a life of comparative ease. But it was not to be. The War Office had paid millions out for their horses, and they wanted their pound of flesh in return; so the horses were cast, which meant a C was branded on their shoulders, to show they were no longer fit for military service and had to be disposed of. In France the draught and transport horses were usually sold off to the slaughterhouses for meat or to local farmers for work on the land.

The lot of the cast riding horse was even more pathetic. His forelegs had gone, so he was no good for riding, and he wasn't strong enough to pull a cart; so off he'd go to an auction with a string of other deadbeats. S. Galtray, in *The Horse and the War*, drew a most poignant picture:

> The pace is funereal, the head of every horse drooping, because you can't hurry the lame, the blind, the broken winded. The onlooker notices the knifeboard back, the staring ribs, the sunken amble of the incredibly lame.
>
> At the sale the buyers move in hoping the army has made a mistake in casting a good 'un. The auctioneer does his best listing merits, as one old wreck after another shambles across the ring causing guffaws of laughter.

Horse slaughterers could afford to pay a better price because meat was desperately short.

Far worse was in store for the brave horses in Palestine. All 20,000 were cast and sold in Egypt. There were howls of protest from the British living in Cairo, from the R.S.P.C.A. and particularly from Major-General Sir George Barrow, G.O.C. of the Yeomanry Division, that the Egyptians were impossibly cruel to animals, that the horses would be starved and flogged to death in the streets, or even more cruelly put to work in the stone quarries.

All protests were to no avail. The official excuse was

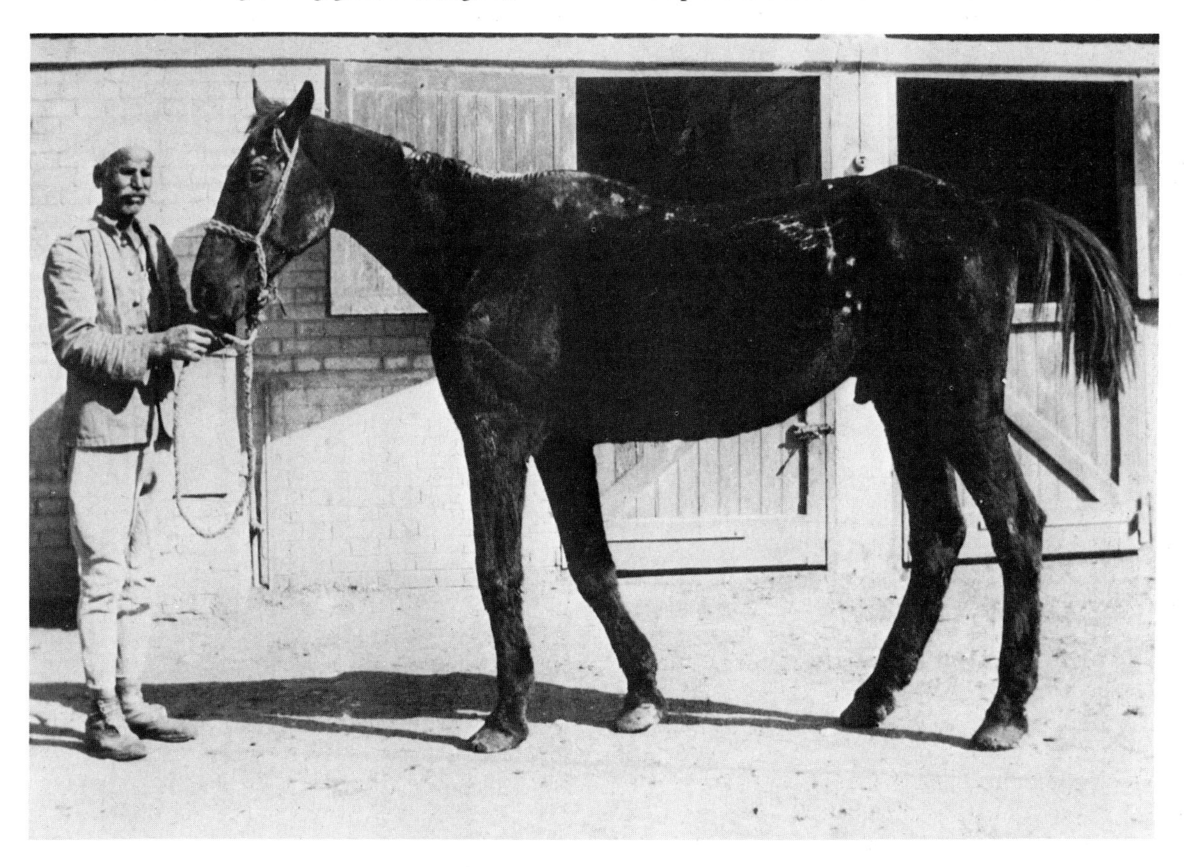

How the British repaid those horses who fought so gallantly in the Desert Campaign. Mrs Brooke found this victim slaving in a stone quarry in Cairo.

that as we had pressed Egypt's camels into military service, it was only fair to sell them back our horses in return. The real truth was cash. The Egyptians would pay £11. 1s. 6d for a horse; if it were destroyed it would only fetch £1.

It was the good General Barrow who looked the other way when the officers of the Desert Mounted Corps took their favourite chargers far out in the desert and shot them. The rest of the horses were sold into slavery – a fine reward for such heroic service.

It makes me proud of my own sex that one courageous woman championed the cause of these wretched horses, though not until eleven years later. In 1930, Dorothy Brooke went to live in Cairo, and was horrified to see the virtual skeletons of British and Australian horses shuffling through the streets. She then proceeded to visit stone quarries, and found the horses there in an even more pitiful state: 'always hungry, weak, overloaded to a degree, lame, crippled, galled, ill-shod, frequently blind, suffering from

Dorothy Brooke in Cairo with some of the ex-British Army horses she rescued.

perpetual thirst, tormented by flies ... straining under the whip.'

Several of the worst cases she rescued out of her own pocket. She then wrote a letter to the *Morning Post*, pointing out the plight of the horses and enclosing a photograph of one of the starved wrecks she had saved, asking for money. The British public was moved, and a flood of cheques poured in. During the next few years, horse lovers all over the world subscribed £40,000. Stables were found, vets employed. Some 5,000 ex-army horses were rescued, many so pulled down they had to be destroyed but the rest enjoyed a peaceful end to their days.

Happily in France, some of the horses that had survived the war found their way home to England, and proudly wore their campaign medals on their bridles when they went hunting. The *Daily Chronicle* also had a nice story of one horse, owned by a Bedfordshire farmer, who had been called up during the war to his master's great distress. Two years later, he was brought back to England, unknown to his old master, and sold to yet another Bedfordshire farmer. One can imagine his first master's delight and amazement when he suddenly heard a clattering of hoofs and imperious neighing in the middle of the night, and looking out saw his old friend poking his head over the gate, demanding to be let in.

One of the reasons the Germans lost World War I was because they ran out of horses. The Allies gained control of the seas, and prevented their enemies importing any more remounts. The Germans, unlike the British, learn by their mistakes. Possibly influenced by the Spanish Civil War, where motorised units were frequently hampered by breakdowns, they began buying up horses. Between 1933 and 1940, the Germans' horse strength rose from 35,000 to 100,000. In fact, many of the horses pulling ammunition and galloping about at Dunkirk were ironically seen to have British First World War brandings.

The English, on the other hand, despite the complaints of a vociferous anti-tank school, gradually scrapped all their cavalry horses, and were the first country in the world to have a completely mechanised army. In 1939, the Secretary of State for War was asked in the House whether mechanisation hadn't been too hasty, and was he aware that the Germans were busy buying our horses? He replied that two regular and sixteen yeomanry cavalry regiments were to be retained as horsed units – in addition to the Life Guards and the Royal Horse Artillery. In fact when war broke out there were only eight yeomanry regiments left.

Where war is concerned, the British are often like a foolish housewife, who as soon as she buys a washing-up machine, promptly chucks away her washing-up bowl and Fairy Liquid. It never enters her head that the machine will break down, or that there will be occasions when the bowl would be more handy to wash up a few fragile cups and saucers.

As it was, as soon as war began, the usual shambles prevailed. It was suddenly decided that 9,000 horses were urgently needed in Palestine. But not only was there a desperate shortage of horses, but also of saddles, farriers, and veterinary staff. A depot was hastily set up on Doncaster racecourse, which had stable room for 600 horses, and could train 175 men at the same time. Three months' veterinary supplies had to be hastily assembled, and 9,000 horses (mostly requisitioned hunters), bought by a remount department, that was sadly lacking in experience. Consequently the units were soon complaining bitterly of the number of too young, too old or unsound horses that were being foisted on them, which had to be packed straight off to hospital.

Then began a nightmarish 2,500 mile journey to Palestine by sea and land, crossing France during the worst winter it had had for years. The horses travelled and must have frozen in open First World War wagons. There were 722 casualties, with 140 deaths from exhaustion, injuries, shippon fever and pneumonia. The sea journey was even worse; one of the transports ran into heavy gales. According to Veterinary Officer J.O. Clabby, who was later to write the official history of R.A.V.C.:

> Most of the men were sea sick, and the horses ankle deep in water. The deck was a shambles, loose horses sliding about on their haunches. One horse had been flung into the donkey

One of the last tasks for British warhorses: a troop of Blues patrols through a village in Palestine in September 1940. LC

engine, and sustained multiple fractures, two horses had broken legs, one fractured its ribs. Having disposed of the badly injured horses, we tied the legs of the remaining horses and lashed them to the rail or mast with sacks under their heads to keep them from drowning, but on this deck and the after tween deck, which was also flooded, horses went down as fast as they got up.

In 1940 some 8,000 horses arrived in Palestine and were formed into the First Cavalry Division, which consisted of the eight remaining mounted yeomanry regiments, and a composite regiment of the Household Cavalry together with Horse Artillery and Signals. The constant movements of its patrols across country and throughout remote areas did much to maintain local peace and security.

Gradually, however, the regiments were mechanised until only two, the Cheshire Yeomanry and the Queen's Own Yorkshire Dragoons, were left. These two had the unenviable duty of fighting our former allies the Vichy French in Syria, but there was not much action. The only enemy villagers that looked like putting up any resistance fled in panic when charged by the Cheshire Yeomanry. In the same operation, a troop of Yorkshire Dragoons were engaged in a skirmish which many believe was our last ever mounted engagement.

After these first three days, until the end of the campaign, the two regiments merely acted as mounted patrols. Once the Syrian campaign was over the Cheshire Yeomanry lost their horses, and the Yorkshire Dragoons only kept theirs until March 1942.

Lt.-Col. D.E. Williams, commanding officer of the Cheshire Yeomanry, describes the splendid exit of the Yorkshire Dragoons. 'There was no actual farewell mounted parade, but the whole regiment, all ranks, had a mounted cross-country race of four miles, which finished with swimming the Jordan. I cannot find out who was the winner, as this seems rather obscure, however, it was very much enjoyed by all.'

But if Britain gave up her horses, other countries did not. In France too the cavalry dream still lingered on. A French friend of the distinguished military commentator Captain Basil Liddell Hart told him, that in 1940 he begged the High Command there that he might be allowed to fell the trees across the forest road leading to the Meuse, and cover this approach with mines to stop German tanks advancing. He was firmly told that the way must be left clear for the advance of the French cavalry. This cavalry duly pushed on to the Ardennes and confronted the Germans, but retreated far more rapidly, routed and with the German Panzers hard on its heels.

In Russia, where frost and snow could always bring tanks and lorries to a halt, the horse was still the basis of the army's transport. In fact, in World War II it had 1,200,000 horses in the field, including thirty cavalry divisions. Once again thousands of them froze and starved to death.

According to J.M. Brereton, one of the last full-scale cavalry charges in history occurred in November 1941, during the German thrust on Moscow, near the village of Musino.

The German 106th Infantry Division supported by the 107th Artillery Division were awaiting orders to move on, when they were astonished to see squadrons of horses debauch from a belt of wood in front of them, and approach at a gallop with drawn swords. When they were about half a mile away, the Germans opened fire, only a handful of about 30 horses reached them, and were gunned down with machine gun fire. In ten minutes, 2,000 horses and their riders of the 44th Mongolian Cavalry Division lay dead and dying in the bloodstained snow, not a single German was hurt.

Even today with the threat of the nuclear bomb ever hovering, countries like China, the Soviet Union, India, Pakistan and South Africa still use the horse to patrol their threatened frontiers. Recently in the Falklands, British soldiers have been using horses to police the snow-bound hills where no army truck can go. In England we still have our Royal Army Veterinary Corps with their 363 acres of rolling green pastureland at Melton Mowbray. Here remounts in chestnut, grey, bay, brown, and black are brought for customers including the Household Cavalry Regiment, The King's Troop, Royal Horse Artillery, HQ The Household Division, the Royal Military Police, the Royal Marines, and the Army School of Equitation. The Veterinary Corps breaks in horses for the

The King's Troop Royal Horse Artillery in practice.

latter three only. The occasional piebald or skewbald is also purchased for Drum Horses.

From here the horses go down to the King's Troop at St John's Wood to be trained to take part in those dashing artillery displays that thrill audiences all over the country but which are still fraught with danger. During one Royal Tournament display for Princess Diana's wedding, while the teams were executing a figure of eight, one gun carriage clipped the back of another, overturning both in a terrifying jumble of horses and riders; and two horses had to be destroyed.

It was on the journey down to another of these displays at Aldershot in June 1982 that the convoy of horseboxes had to do a U-turn on the motorway and hurtle back to London under police escort to fire the gun salute in Hyde Park to tell the people of London that the Princess of Wales had given birth to a son.

And the feeling of the Royal Artillery soldier for his horse today is the same as it was in the trenches. As one officer said: 'He would murder his grandmother, leave his wife, punch up his fellow soldier, rifle his mother's handbag, rather than let a hair of his horse's head be harmed.'

It was at Melton Mowbray that I first met Sefton

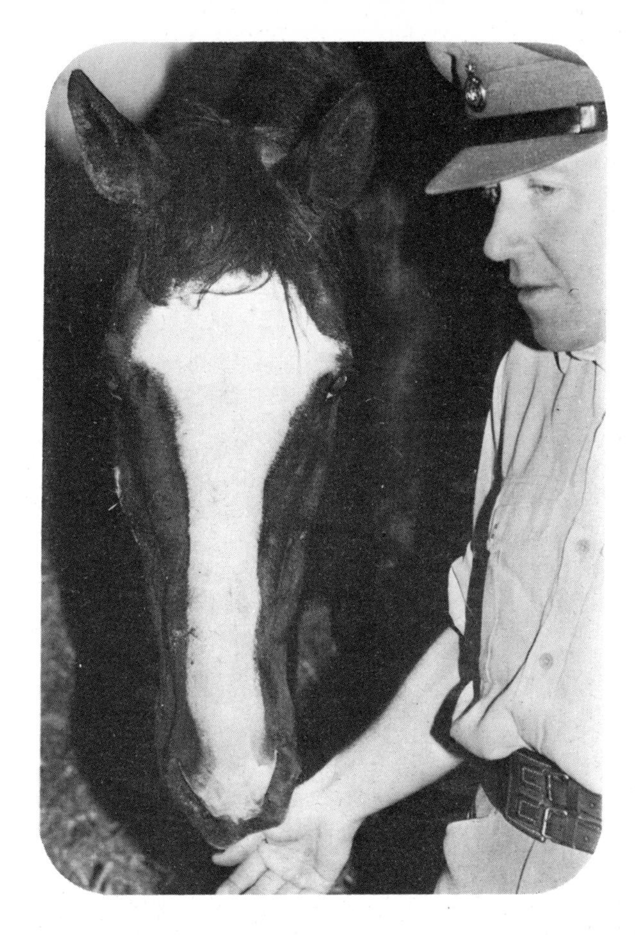

Sefton, at nineteen the oldest equine survivor of the Hyde Park bombing in June 1982, was also the most severely injured. He received thousands of presents and get well soon cards, and became a national symbol of courage. (BY COURTESY OF *THE MAIL ON SUNDAY*)

and the other seven Household Cavalry horses about seven weeks after their terrible ordeal in Hyde Park. There was Bandit, covered in scars, who kicked anyone who went behind him; and Quo Minus, known as Jimmy, who was always kept in the stable, because he shivered with cold every time they put him out in the field; and Eclipse, who had a nail piercing him that had to be wound out like a corkscrew. In the tackroom, the get-well cards and presents of carrots, and barley sugar and mints were piled to the ceiling. Most of them were for Sefton, who lapped up all the attention, obviously realising he had become a star. The other horses jumped when a gate was slammed too hastily, but not Sefton. His wise old head with its wide white blaze looked out over the green door. The scars on his pitted body were healing well, and as I put my arms round his neck, for a minute he rested his velvet whiskery chin against my shoulder. 'I'm sorry,' I whispered, 'for what's been done to you, and all the millions and millions of other horses down the ages.' And suddenly I understood the courage and philosophical acceptance that has sustained him and all the million others, as he began gently to nudge at my coat pocket in search of his favourite barley sugar.

The Golden Tail

'Phoebus Apollo heard his prayer and came down in a fury . . . he attacked the mules first, and the nimble dogs; then he aimed his sharp arrows at the men and struck again and again. Day and night innumerable fires consumed the dead.'

Homer: THE ILIAD *translated by E.V. Rieu*

No animal has served man more nobly in war than the dog. Guarding outposts, detecting mines, racing messages through an inferno of gunfire – he acted out of love, not because he was made to. He is the only animal who can be trusted to think for himself. It is tragic that the numerous services he had to offer were so often rejected and derided by the authorities.

In the years leading up to World War I, most European countries built up military dog training schools. Germany had been experimenting with dogs since 1870, subsidising a network of village clubs which specialised in breeding and training dogs for army work. Even more ironically, the Germans had steadily been buying up the best British breeds, so that when war broke out, they had 6,000 dogs straining at the leash for active service. The British had one: an Airedale who went to France as a guard dog with the Second Battalion, Norfolk Regiment and was killed in action on the Aisne.

Britain, in fact, was the last country to set up a war dog school, and then only because of the heroic persistence of Lt.-Col. E.H. Richardson, a well-known dog trainer. Having been repeatedly snubbed by the War Office, he finally convinced them that so many despatch carriers were being killed at the front, that it would be worth trying out dogs as messengers.

At last in 1916, he was asked to set up an official dog training school. Within a week, the gallant colonel and his wife (who like him was a genius with animals) had shut up their house, stored their furniture, and moved to Shoeburyness in Essex. Here, on the coast near the watery marshes, and within the sound of the bombardment, they set to work.

Their first problem was to find suitable dogs. Many came from the Dog Homes, which, because of the shortage of food, were overflowing. The public were also asked to lend their dogs. Gloomy about the response, the War Office laid on a skeleton staff. Within a few days, they were buckling under offers from more than 7,000 owners. Many of the letters were heartbreaking:

'My husband has gone, my son has gone,' wrote one woman. 'Please take my dog to bring this cruel war to an end.'

Whilst the British Expeditionary Force marched everywhere on foot the local population, whose dogs had been commandeered, used dogs instead to help out. This picture was probably taken in 1914. IWM

The War Dog Training School, Shoeburyness, Essex – World War I. IWM

One patriotic little girl wrote: 'We have let Daddy go and fight the Kaiser, now we are sending Jack to do his bit.'

Owners might not have been quite so willing to lend their beloved pets, if they'd realised one of the first tests they'd have to endure. The dogs were fed once a day. Three minutes before feeding time, very noisy grenades were thrown into a pit nearby, making an appalling din. For a few days after the dogs arrived,

nothing would induce them to come out of their kennels during the bombing, and as the food was removed the moment the bombing stopped, they had to go hungry. Little by little, hunger overcame fear. Within a week, dogs who were going to be any good were straining at their leads as the first bomb exploded – the rest were sent back to their owners, or to the Dogs Home to be put down.

The next step in the training was for each of Lt.-Col. Richardson's staff to lead three dogs a few hundred yards away from the kennels, and put a slip of paper into a leather pouch on each dog's collar stating the time and distance. The dogs were then set free, and sped back to the kennels where Lt.-Col. Richardson, whom they now regarded as master, was waiting to make much of them and reward them with bits of chopped liver. Every day the distance was increased. The dogs were also trained to run through busy towns,

Lieutenant-Colonel E.H. Richardson, who set up the school for military dogs during World War I. IWM

past burning haystacks, through cruel entangled nests of barbed wire, and to ignore bursts of shell and machine gun fire. Soon they were racing home from four or five miles away.

The dogs, like children, were immensely competitive and loved to show off. Sometimes two rivals would stop to have a fight on the way. One dog once arrived looking very sheepish, having pinched a workman's lunch wrapped in a pocket handkerchief. When they raced in, all the dogs not employed on that particular run, would stand on their kennels barking encouragement.

After only a month, the dogs were considered ready for the front. Three dogs were allocated to each handler, to whom they'd already got very attached. When they reached the front, the procedure was for a soldier to take the dogs forward where the fighting was. They were then given water, but no food, and as soon as the troops needed to send a message, saying perhaps that they were running short of ammunition, the dog was despatched. Off he would tear, through a terrible barrage of shots and shell fire, often belly-deep in mud, back to his beloved handler, who after passing on the important information, would reward the dog with praise and a large dinner.

The advantage of the messenger dog was that he could bring messages through three times faster than a man. He was also less of a target for the enemy, and in bad conditions he was light enough to creep round the rim of a shell hole. If he fell in, not being weighed down by bulky gear, he could swim across. When the telephone wires were down, and it was too dark for signalling, and too foggy or wet or dark, for pigeons, dogs were the only things that got through.

And how seriously they took their duties. One Australian officer, seeing a Welsh terrier 'running, hopping, jumping, skipping over the terrible shell holes,' was impressed by the 'earnest expression on the dog's face as he passed'.

Many dogs battled on when they were badly gassed or wounded. Only after a post mortem was it discovered that one dog had been carrying messages for weeks with a bullet in his lungs and a piece of shrapnel imbedded in his spine.

Mrs Richardson with pupils. IWM

Dog leaping a trench while taking back a message. The message carrier attached to the collar can easily be seen. Near Sedan, May 1917. IWM

Then there was the French messenger dog, Von Kluck, captured from the Germans and named after one of the leading German field commanders. One day, an officer waiting for an urgent message, saw the dog apparently dawdling and yelled at him to buck up. Von Kluck rallied gallantly, then seemed to go even slower. A few minutes later, he staggered in and collapsed dead at the officer's feet.

Perhaps the most heroic messenger dog, was Satan, the halfbreed black greyhound, who helped to save a vital position at Verdun. His handler, Duvalle, was biting his nails in a corner of the beleaguered town, which was fast running out of ammunition and being relentlessly smashed to bits by a German battery to the right. Suddenly Duvalle, who'd been continually scanning the horizon for help, saw a black speck

This messenger dog has all four paws burned by mustard gas but still manages to keep smiling. IWM

streaking towards them across no man's land. It was Satan, shifting so fast that some of the French soldiers thought he had wings. Next minute the dog buckled, and crashed to the ground, hit by a bullet. Immediately Duvalle stood suicidally up on the trench wall in full view of the enemy.

'Courage, Satan, mon ami,' he yelled, 'Viens pour la France,' and was mown down by a hail of bullets. Brave Satan, however, hearing his beloved master's voice, staggered to his feet, and with his shattered back leg hanging, struggled the last few hundred yards, bringing a message to the town to hang on, because help was at hand. On his back, too, were not wings, but baskets containing two terrified carrier pigeons. These were immediately despatched with a message to the French line, telling them to wipe out the German battery to the right. One pigeon was killed on the way; the other struggled through; the battery was silenced; a crucial corner of Verdun was saved.

Although many British dogs were given the chance to carry vital information back from the front, it was tragic that as many others were written off as a waste of time. Success depended very much on the battery commander, many of whom were too busy or too exhausted to bother with dogs. Some ignored the poor animals, some openly laughed at them, or worst of all set them impossible tasks to prove they were useless.

Another problem was that the dog-loving British soldier rather spread himself in kind attentions to the visiting dogs, feeding them and petting them when they were up at the front. This, of course, was fatal from the training point of view, as it took the dog's mind off his handler and his dinner back at the base.

A glance through the messenger dog record book at the Imperial War Museum shows the appalling wastage. Nellie, Dick and Jock, for example, were all given away described as 'no use to the service'. Three collies, Nell, Cosy and Surefoot, and two lurchers, King and Sea, were all shot 'for being useless'. Charlie, a King Charles Spaniel (goodness knows what a gentle timid dog like that was doing at the front) was also 'shot by O.C. for being useless'. The list goes on.

One wonders how many owners, who had so innocently and trustingly lent their dogs in the hope of getting them back after the war ever realised what tragic ends they met. They would no doubt have been tempted to shoot the O.C. in his turn for being 'useless'.

It was poignant, too, the way the handlers in their stilted reports sent home to Lt.-Col. Richardson, cherished any tiny crumb of praise from their superiors writing with pride of 'the wonderful run Jack made with an important message when nothing else could get through,' or Tommy 'who made it though badly gassed.'

'Dogs did great work during advance in Nieppe forest,' wrote one handler. 'The G.O.C., 88th Brigade, wrote out and had a note typed giving praise to Jock, Bruno, and Champion. That was the first official praise we had from anyone.'

In the Second World War matters improved and a record of all dogs entered into the Army was kept, and all dogs were offered back to their owners at the end of hostilities.

Lt.-Col. Richardson, on the whole, found Airedales, collies, lurchers and whippets made the best messenger dogs. But some breeds defeated him. Hounds were too independent; poodles and fox terriers, too frivolous.

He also wrote: 'I have rarely found a dog with a gay tail, which curled over its back or sideways of any use. It seems to indicate a certain levity of character, quite at variance with the serious duties required.'

The Colonel also trained many dogs to guard ammunition dumps, factories, top secret research stations, and above all as sentries. It was common practice in World War I for both sides to mount raids to capture enemy soldiers in order to obtain information. The presence of guard dogs did much to inhibit this; and once soldiers were armed with a guard dog, the practice usually ceased abruptly. It is interesting too that the breeds Lt.-Col. Richardson found made the best guard dogs: setters, Great Danes, deerhounds and Irish wolfhounds, are those we today would regard as the most gentle.

The French tended to employ huge shaggy sheepdogs called Chiens de Brie as guard dogs, which they

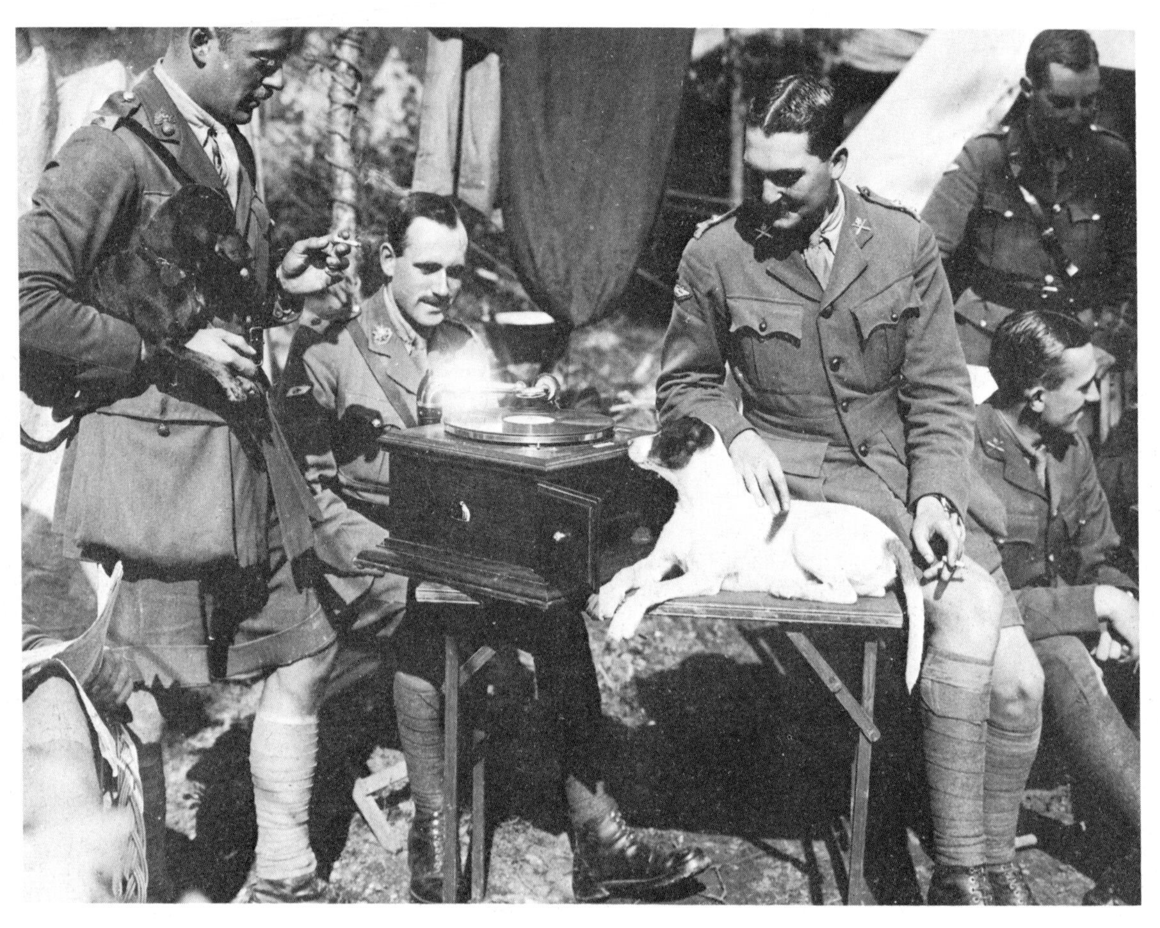

trained at a big kennel in the Vosges. Lt.-Col. Richardson tells a touching story in his book *Fifty Years with Dogs*, of one of these dogs who performed his duties most conscientiously but always with a wistful faraway look in his eyes. He must have been worrying about his sheep back in his farm in Avignon, because one day he went missing, and the French soldiers, who'd become very fond of him, were delighted a fortnight later to hear he'd tramped all the 300 miles home. Happily, it was felt he'd done his duty towards the war effort, and he was allowed to stay in Avignon and tend his sheep.

Dogs had many other duties in the First World War. In Belgium, everything was pressed into service, including the country's staunch draught dogs to pull the machine guns. A Belgian officer said what a pathetic sight it was to see civilians telling the soldiers their pets' names and eating habits, listing their funny little ways, and begging that they should be kindly treated and returned when the war was over. Sadly, many of them were killed and wounded at Liège and Namur, as their work was very dangerous. An officer rushing forward would select a suitable gun position. When he gave the signal, the dogs would leap up and race the gun carriages towards him at full gallop. The gun would then be lifted off and set in the firing line while another soldier rushed the dogs to safety. The Belgian gunners grew very attached to their solid,

Dogs were set to many different tasks during World War I.
Facing Page: *'Their masters' voices' – tank officers and their pets at Poperinghe in September 1917. This dachshund (left) fared better than many of his breed who suffered on account of their German origins.*
Below left: *French carrier dog and his load of grenades pictured at the Military Kennel at Camp de Santony, May 1918.*
Below right: *Laying telegraph wire on the Western Front.* All IWM

stumpytailed dogs, groomed them every day, and slept with them lying across their legs, for warmth at night.

Other dogs were trained to carry ammunition and, when communications had broken down, lay telephone cables across no man's land, unrolling minute reels on their backs. The plethora of corpses on the Western Front, also produced plagues of rats which acquired a taste for human flesh.

This made life unbearable for the men in the trenches and dugouts, but fortunately tough terriers were invaluable allies in their war against the rats, and often notched up individual scores as high as the flying aces.

The Italians employed large dogs to pull supplies over the Alps. Clambouring up crevices where no horse could go, light enough not to break the crusting of the snow, a squad of dogs could between them draw a ton of mail, ammunition, light guns, food or medical supplies. The Italians were devoted to these canine teams, giving a rousing cheer when they arrived at their destination. The dogs had the same food as the soldiers, coffee and bread for breakfast, broth, meat, bread and water for lunch, and meat, bread, sugar and chocolate for dinner.

Between the wars, our messengers and guard dog services were disbanded, and while the Soviet Union, Japan, Germany and most other countries built up their canine armies, Britain and France – the perennial

Dog as ammunition carrier: 'Mark' delivers Lewis Gun rounds to a section of British troops in the Eastern Command area. Mark was given to the B.E.F. by the 1st French Army and was on active service from November 1939 to 1 June 1940. IWM

foolish virgins – let theirs lapse. Once again Lt.-Col. Richardson tried to galvanise the War Office, but the usual buckpassing prevailed. Everyone pointed out to him that this was now a mechanical age, that we were fighting a war of movement, and that anyway radio had made messenger dogs obsolete.

It was not until war broke out and reports started flooding in of recce patrols not functioning according to plan, of outposts being surprised, and ammunition dumps broken into, that it was decided that perhaps dogs were needed after all. The Greyhound Racing kennels at Potter's Bar, were therefore commandeered in 1942, and the Army War Dog School set up.

The threat of bombing had led to 400,000 dogs and cats in the London area alone being destroyed in the first few weeks of the war. As a result, there was a distinct dearth of healthy dogs, and once again the public were asked to lend their pets. Of 10,000 patriotically offered, only 3,500 were accepted. The majority were trained as guard dogs, and saved the country millions of pounds protecting ammunition dumps, aerodromes, and prisoner of war camps. The efforts of the guard dog usually go unsung, because it is his duty to act as a deterrent, and no one can assess the number of intruders he has frightened off, though a Boxer called Simmi had eighty-six arrests to his credit in Palestine during World War II and was officially praised for the 'wholehearted' way he carried out his duties.

Occasionally guard dogs could be a little overzeal-

During a lull in the fighting on the Pacific volcanic island of Iwo Jima in 1945, a U.S. Marine snatches a moment of sleep in a foxhole while his guard dog keeps watch. IWM

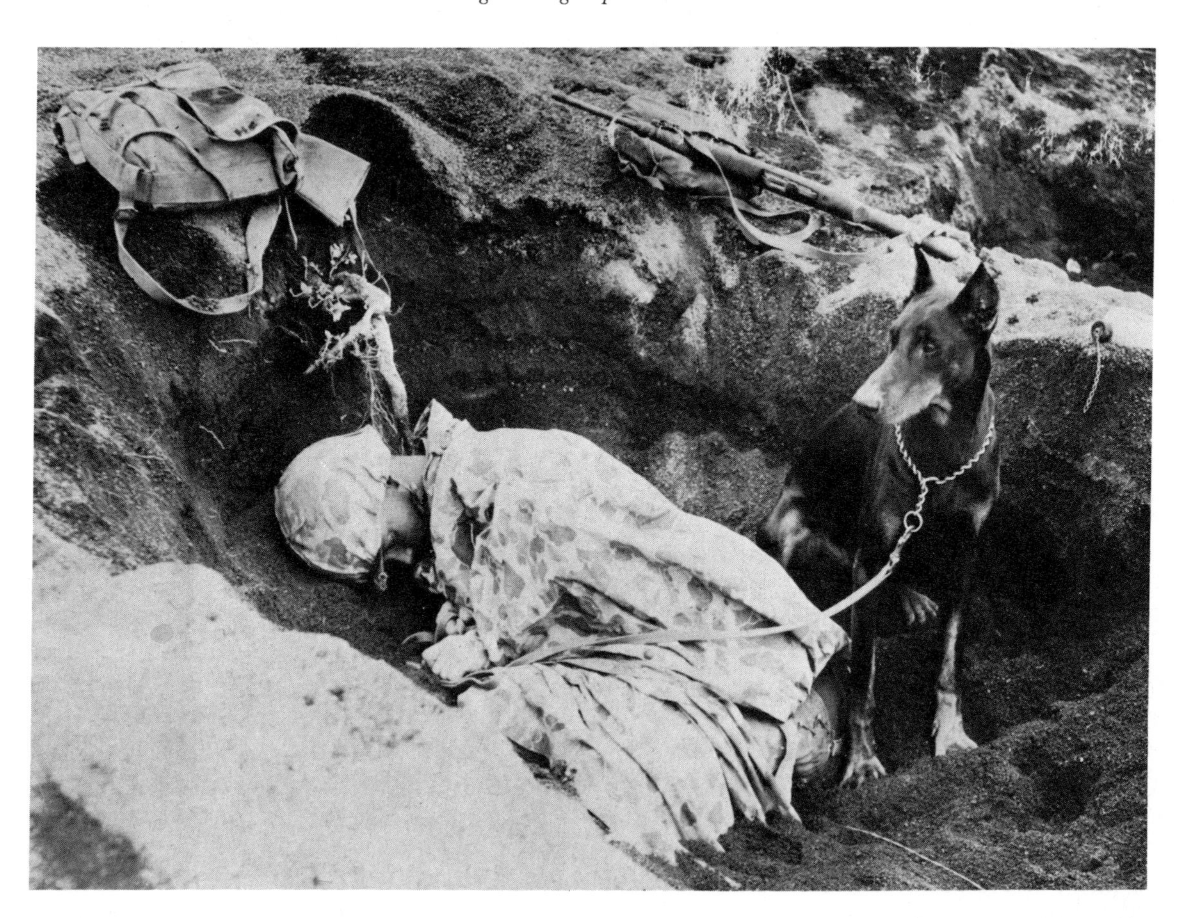

ous. One handler working for a radio station heard unauthorised footsteps, and let loose his dog. Next moment he heard a piercing shriek, and racing round the corner, found one of the announcers, who'd taken advantage of a break in transmission to go for a stroll, clinging halfway up a pylon, with the dog snarling furiously below. The BBC had to apologise profusely for a technical hitch.

In the First World War, the dog most widely employed in military service was the Airedale. In World War II, he was supplanted by the Alsatian, whose strength, courage, alertness, superb intelligence, and passionate unswerving devotion to his handler, make him the ideal dog of war. So great has been his success, that of all the dogs trained at the R.A.V.C. headquarters in Melton Mowbray for war work today, 80 per cent are Alsatians.

On account of his undeniable courage, the bull terrier was also tried out as a guard dog. He was rejected not only because his coat was too thin to stand cold weather, but also because of his wilful nature. One very wet, very cold night, a bull terrier guard dog deserted his handler for the comforts of the guardroom fire, and resisted all persuasion to resume his duties.

The Dickin Medal, donated by the People's Dispensary for Sick Animals, is engraved with the words 'For gallantry, we also serve'. The colours of the ribbons are green, brown, and pale blue to symbolise valour on sea, land and sky. The animals' V.C., it was only awarded for exceptional bravery. On several occasions

The Dickin Medal was awarded by the P.D.S.A. and engraved with the words 'For Gallantry, We also Serve'. The animal kingdom's VC, it was only awarded for exceptional bravery. Judy's medal is pictured here. IWM

Rob, known as the 'paradog', made over twenty parachute landings and won a Dickin Medal. IWM

the medal was won by patrol dogs, who in World War II were trained to lead little groups of soldiers into no-man's land, sniff out the enemy, and give silent warning and direction to the patrol. Bob, a crossbred collie, attached to C. Company of the 6th Queen's Own Royal West Kent Regiment, went with the regiment to North Africa in 1943 where he won the Dickin Medal at Green Hill. With his white patches camouflaged with dark paint, he led a night patrol into enemy lines. Suddenly he froze in his tracks. The patrol waited, then hearing nothing, ignored the dog's warning, and decided to push on. Bob stood his ground; a second later, the enemy was sighted 200 yards ahead, much nearer than anyone realised. Bob had saved the patrol from almost certain capture or death, and they were able to retreat to safety, with valuable information.

Rob, another mongrel, black and white with a piratical patch over one eye, served with the S.A.S. taking part in landings in North Africa and then in Italy. Most of his work was highly dangerous. Known as the 'para dog' he made over twenty parachute landings, which he seemed to relish, jumping out of the plane without a moment's hesitation. Reaching the ground, he lay still, until his handler caught up with him, and removed his parachute. Rob was once dropped with an S.A.S. party behind enemy lines, where they remained for many months. They faced incredible dangers, and Rob never failed to guard the party. After such an ordeal it was hardly surprising Rob was not overawed by the aristocracy and shook paws in a matey fashion, with Viscount De L'Isle and Dudley, when presented by him with his Dickin Medal.

Often things went wrong. Bing, an Alsatian, dropped into Normandy on D-Day with the 13th battalion of the Parachute Regiment, landed in a tree, and was shelled by the enemy until he was rescued next morning. Although wounded in the neck and eyes, he was completely undaunted, and immediately took his place with his handler in the line. The battalion was perilously close to the enemy, the right flank resting in a thick wood. Through very heavy bombardment, Bing stood guard on this vital section of the battalion's

Salvo, who was owned by 2nd Lt. Hugh Fletcher, was No. 1 applicant for the 'Parapup Battalion', at Andrews Field somewhere in England. Here he is seen descending. IWM

Mine-sniffing dogs used in France after the Normandy invasion. Note the white tapes laid to keep the search in line.
IWM

front. His presence was a great comfort to the troops, particularly at night.

The real brainchild of World War II, however, was the mine dog. The only animals included in the British invasion force were the guard dogs of the military police, the few patrol dogs of the Parachute Regiment, and the mine detecting dogs of the Sappers. In July 1944, four platoons of the latter were posted to northwest Europe. For six months, they worked every day; in Holland alone, they checked 100 miles of railway. They were trained to sit down the instant they picked up the smell of a mine.

Quite one of the bravest mine dogs was a beautiful Welsh sheepdog called Ricky. He was clearing a canal bank in Holland when, in the middle of the exercise, one of the mines, though detected, blew up three feet away from him, killing the section commander, and wounding poor Ricky in the face. With remarkable fortitude, he didn't panic, continued his task of finding several more mines, and won himself a Dickin Medal in the process.

Mine dogs were far more effective than the metal detector, in that they could detect mines made of plastic, wood, and glass (as well as metal), and also recognise when earth had been recently dug up. Occasionally, like hounds who don't find a fox, they got bored if they searched too long without discovering a mine. But on the whole they thoroughly enjoyed the work, and got as wildly excited when their harnesses were put on as a gun dog at the prospect of a day's shooting.

The Russians also used mine dogs extensively. One mongrel, called Zucha, on one occasion found 2,000 mines in eighteen days. So important were his services that when an aerodrome needed clearing he always arrived by plane with his master. Within a few hours, the area would be rendered safe.

Dickin Medal winner Ricky, one of the bravest mine dogs, carried on undeterred when a mine blew up and wounded him as he was clearing a canal bank in Holland.

Americans also did much work with mine dogs, and during the Vietnam War, trained them to detect the hideous ambushes and eye and groin level booby traps of the Viet Cong. Unlike the British, who reward their dogs with titbits, the Americans used the repulsion method, giving the dog an electric shock every time he found a mine, which taught him to proceed with caution but not to locate the exact position of the mine. As a result, American dogs tended not to be as successful as ours. Attempting to clear some mines in Korea, the Americans tried a group of golden retrievers and basset hounds but only returned a poor 10 per cent success. The bassets were particularly inept, refusing to take their duties remotely seriously. In the end the Americans gave up and drove sheep back and forth across the mined areas.

In 1982, the R.A.V.C. spent several months training dogs to detect unexploded mines laid by the Argentinians in the Falkland Islands. By November they were returning a 100 per cent success rate. But in one appallingly difficult test, with the ground under 2 inches of water to simulate Falklands conditions, they found only 70 per cent of the mines, which was not considered good enough to send them out. Nevertheless, as this book goes to press they are being kept in reserve. One cannot help selfishly hoping they will not be subjected to such dangerous and trying work.

In attempting to find more efficient mine detectors, the Americans have tried out pigs, coyotes, cats, racoons, skunks, deer, ferrets and dogs of many different crosses. Pigs were easily the best; not for nothing had they been sniffing out truffles in the Périgord forests for centuries. But what soldier would be seen leading a pig through the streets to clear a suspected minefield? Dogs, of course, have been outstandingly successful in Northern Ireland, sniffing out explosives, weapons and ammunition, tracking terrorists and also dispersing riots. In February 1974, after thirty hooligans had been stoning troops at a housing estate near Palace Barracks, they were seen off in no time, by one Alsatian and his handler.

Dogs have also been responsible for uncovering a great deal of terrorist equipment, including wirelesses, batteries, uniform, and subversive literature (the dogs themselves would probably put the works of Barbara Woodhouse in that category).

Occasionally even the most responsible dogs fall from grace. During a nationwide terrorist hunt, a sniffer bloodhound suddenly became wildly excited. On being released, he took off over a nearby wall, only to return five minutes later with a large sheep in his mouth.

All the dogs in the British army today are graduates from the R.A.V.C. centre at Melton Mowbray, which aims to train 320 dogs and 600 handlers a year, and has 13,000 ex-pupils doing sterling work in trouble spots all over the world.

Carrying on the tradition of both world wars, all the dogs trained by the R.A.V.C. are donated by the public or purchased for a nominal fee. Some are given because they are too strong and boisterous. Others are casualties of broken homes, where neither side wants the dog, or victims of inflation, where the family is too poor to keep a large dog with a healthy appetite.

Only dogs, not bitches, are accepted – because the R.A.V.C. believes somewhat chauvinistically that dogs are more robust, aggressive and have more stamina. They are taken between the ages of eighteen months and three years, but an exceptional dog may be accepted earlier.

The new arrivals are a pathetic sight, mostly Alsatians and a few Labradors. They sit licking their lips, whining, continually glancing at the door, hoping by some miracle that their owners are coming back to collect them, just like little boys on their first day at prep school. Fortunately, the kennel maids from the W.R.A.C. are devoted to the dogs, and spend a lot of time mothering the new boys to make them feel at home.

Within a week or so they are transformed animals, bouncing with energy and health, barking their heads off to show how bold and aggressive they've become. Meanwhile, the inmates who've been there a few months and who are about to graduate, perhaps to Germany or Hong Kong, or Northern Ireland, lounge around looking superior like school prefects or members of the first eleven, conserving any barking or ferocity for when it matters.

Around the corner from the training yards, is a row of empty houses known as Harley Street, where specialist dogs are trained to track down arms and explosives. Booby traps are put behind ventilators, and hidden under door mats and window ledges. Stairs and chairs come apart to reveal arms caches. 'The dog,' explained Sergeant-Major Aylward of the R.A.V.C., 'is trained to search the room on his own, and then go round with his handler on a lead. The handler has to learn every mood, expression and nose twitch of his dog. If he keeps indicating at a particular spot, you must undo the wall even if you know there's nothing there, just to show you've got faith in him.'

Experienced dogs also have the laborious task of training new handlers. In another field, a very hot and bothered soldier was being initiated into the mysteries of dog handling by a very wise old Alsatian. The dog had a resigned, but somewhat martyred expression on his face as he towed his pupil back and forth, as if asking: why should I put up with yet another young idiot on the end of a lead.

'Dogs can be very sarcastic,' said Sergeant-Major Aylward, 'During the first week, they take the micky out of the new boys something terrible.'

But despite the barking, more often as you walk round you hear the heavy thump of a tail on the floorboards as a handler approaches. Great trouble is taken to 'marry up' the right handler to the right dog, and there is no questioning the strength of devotion that grows between them. Recently a handler went on leave for a few days before he and the dog were posted to Germany, but came back early when he heard the dog was pining and refusing to eat.

Dogs also became extremely attached to their handlers in the Second World War. One Alsatian called Judy, when her handler was taken to hospital, strained on her collar until it broke, pawed back the bolt of the dog compound, raced past numerous buildings, she'd never seen before, dashed into the hospital, leapt over two beds and landed in her handler's arms. In twenty-four hours she was taken back to her kennel four times, but each time escaped, making a beeline for her handler's bed.

Working so closely together, it must have been terrible for the handler to give up his dogs when the war ended. Corporal A. McLellan spoke for hundreds of men when he wrote to the P.D.S.A. about his Alsatian Peter:

'I had to accompany him to his owner. When I left, he told me in his own way he wanted to come with me. I had to pat him, and bid him stay. At the word "stay", he lay down and the pathetic look in his eyes, I shall never forget. The tears ran down my cheeks as I patted him again.'

One can also understand the owners longing to have their dogs back again. Ricky the mine dog was so brilliant at his job that the army wanted to pay his owner a large sum to keep him, but this was refused.

One crossbred Alsatian called Dodo joined up at eighteen months and for three years guarded German prisoners of war. His owner, Mr Gooding, was warned not to have the dog back, as he had become very ferocious and could only be controlled by his handler. But Mr Gooding insisted he wanted Dodo home again. With some trepidation he met the dog at the station. At the sight of his old master, Dodo went crazy with delight and back home settled in quietly as though he'd never been away.

No one will ever know how many lives or how much manpower have been saved by our Army dogs, or how much the morale of the troops is boosted by these brave but cheerful and loving companions. Certainly their value is out of all proportion to the small numbers used.

To end on a truly poignant note, perhaps the most heartbreaking task in the Second World War was performed by the Russian suicide dogs. When the Panzer tanks were rolling towards Moscow, and nothing seemed likely to stop them, the Russians trained little mongrels to hurtle under the tanks, carrying a primed bomb strapped on their backs, and crouch there until dog and tank were blown to eternity. It is unbearable to think of that last split second of bewilderment and sense of betrayal that must have flashed through the dogs' minds.

I talked to one Polish General, who said that during the last war Poland was emptied of dogs. They were all taken off to the Soviet Union to join the suicide squads, the Soviet rationale being that it was better to sacrifice a dog's life than a human. One can only reiterate with Luther: 'Be comforted, little dog, thou too in the Resurrection, shall have a little golden tail.'

Homer Sweet Homer

'And he stayed yet another seven days; and again he sent forth the dove out of the ark; And the dove came in to him in the evening, and lo, in her mouth was an olive leaf pluckt off: so Noah knew that the waters were abated from off the earth.'

GENESIS

When my father was working at the War Office during the last war, he seemed to come home every night with a new pigeon joke. My favourite was the one about the male pigeon who fell in love with a female pigeon and arranged to meet her at three o'clock at the bottom of Nelson's column. Arriving on the dot, he waited and waited. Finally at five when he'd given up all hope, the female pigeon sauntered up, saying, 'I'm so sorry I'm late, but it was such a lovely day, I thought I'd walk.'

But while I, and I suspect half England, were revelling in these pigeon jokes, few of us realised the heroic feats being achieved by pigeons, and how many thousands of lives they saved in both world wars.

The use of pigeons in war, in fact, is almost as old as war itself. In 1150 BC, the Sultan of Baghdad had capsules filled with papyrus sheets strapped to the leg or back feathers of a bird. Pigeons relayed the news of Caesar's conquest of Gaul, and the news of Wellington's victory at Waterloo, many days before the official courier. They were also invaluable during the siege of Paris of 1870. Taken by balloon to Tours or London, the birds were then sent back to Paris, with letters for the besieged Parisians. By the aid of photography, messages were copied greatly reduced on to thin films of collodian, which were later relayed on to a screen by magic lantern. On one occasion, one little pigeon carried 40,000 messages, and during the four months of the siege, pigeons brought 150,000 official letters and a million private letters into Paris.

In view of such success, it was inevitable that in 1908 the British Admiralty declared our pigeon service to be obsolete because of the invention of wireless. Despite the fact that both Germany and France were building up well-organised pigeon services, the British Government promptly got rid of all their own pigeons, and at the beginning of World War I, in a frenzy of paranoia about spies, ordered that all private pigeons should be let loose, or interned with their wings clipped. Within a few months, however, it was discovered that most of the mine-sweepers and drifters policing the channel, which were not equipped with wireless, had no means of communicating with the shore, or warning other ships of torpedoes or newly laid mines.

None for the pot.

DEFENCE OF THE REALM

Regulation 21A.

SHOOTING HOMING PIGEONS.

Killing, Wounding or Molesting Homing Pigeons

is punishable under the Defence of the Realm Regulations by

SIX MONTHS IMPRISONMENT OR £100 FINE.

The Public are reminded that Homing Pigeons are doing valuable work for the Government, and are requested to assist in the suppression of the shooting of these birds.

£5 REWARD

will be paid by the NATIONAL HOMING UNION for information leading to the conviction of any person SHOOTINC HOMING PIGEONS the property of its Members.

Information should be given to the Police, Military Post, or to the Secretary of the Union, C. C. PLACKETT, 14, EAST PARADE, LEEDS.

Wm. GILL & Co. (PRINTERS) Ltd., LEEDS.

A mobile pigeon loft on the Western Front. IWM

It was fortunate that another gallant and persistent officer, Captain A.H. Osman had made a study of carrier pigeons and, like Lt.-Col. Richardson with his messenger dogs, had repeatedly tried to persuade the War Office how useful they might be. Now he was on the spot, to marshall pigeon fanciers to turn the other cheek and offer both their birds and their services to the war effort. It was not long before mine sweepers and other ships were sending home valuable messages to a string of pigeon lofts hastily set up along the South and East coasts.

One trawler captain, newly equipped with pigeons, felt after a week or so that he ought to send a message back to base – even if he had nothing of importance to report. He therefore despatched a bird saying, 'All well here, beef pudding for dinner,' a message which passed along all the red tape and finally reached the Admiralty, so the captain was nicknamed Beef Pudding for the rest of the war.

As field telegraph and wireless were always breaking down, pigeons were frequently used at the front. Despatch riders on bicycles took the birds up to the firing line in baskets. As soon as there was anything important to report, say a battalion had advanced too far and had been cut off by the enemy, or a certain part of the line was weak and needed reinforcements, a message was scribbled out and put in a small aluminium container which was then clipped to the pigeon's leg. It was vital to keep the pigeon under cover, as they couldn't fly if their feathers were coated with mud, and not to clip the container too tightly, as this stopped circulation.

Pigeons were set free in duplicate (usually two males or two females, so they didn't indulge in sexual dalliance on the way). They then flew back to their lofts, heard their mates calling, shot through a hinged door that only opened inwards, which rang a bell, and alerted a soldier who rushed the message up to headquarters, or the nearest commanding officer.

The pigeons returned either to a permanent loft at an important centre well behind the lines or to a mobile loft which followed the movements of the fighting forces. In the early days of the war, the mobile lofts were often converted omnibuses pulled by horses, but by the end of the war, they were mostly motorised.

Pigeons had the advantage over dogs in that they were much faster and were not bogged down by mud and shell holes. They also provided a much smaller target, and flew distances of sixty miles without turning a feather, whereas the dog was seldom reliable over more than five miles. Although pigeons detest flying in the dark or in heavy rain or fog, many of them soldiered on through intensive shell fire and gas, with shrapnel or bullets lodged in their breasts, or with beaks or legs blown off, and crashed to their deaths bringing their messages through.

Cher Ami, for example, the well-named blue chequered American pigeon, delivered no fewer than twelve messages and never failed. In her last flight in the Argonne, she lost a leg and struck her pigeon loft breast first, then hopped in on one bloody leg with the tube bearing the message, hanging from the ligament of the leg that had been shot off. A hole through the breastbone had been made by the same bullet, but she still covered 25 miles in the same number of minutes. The message was a vital one from a platoon in desperate trouble. Reinforcements saved the situation and many a posthumous toast was drunk to Cher Ami.

The French also used pigeons extensively. Of the 4,000 despatched at the battle of the Somme, only 2 per cent failed to return, and this was usually because they'd been gassed or shot down. If their pigeons showed unusual gallantry, the French rewarded them with the Croix de Guerre; and because pigeons can't wear medals on their breasts, special bands with the colours of the medal were sewn round their legs.

One Commandant and his battalion were surrounded at Verdun, his last pigeon but one flew through an incredible hailstorm of enemy fire, and received the Croix de Guerre. His last pigeon was badly mangled, dropped dead as he delivered his message, and was awarded the Légion d'Honneur.

Occasionally there were some welcome lighter moments. During one big scale engagement, a pigeon arrived, and everyone gathered round the officer who took the message, which read plaintively, 'I'm fed up with sending blasted messages.' While a Canadian officer despatched a missive from the front, saying,

'Lucky pigeon to get out of this hell of a place.' One Australian battalion, obviously browned off with sending practice pigeon messages, shot off a note which when decoded read, 'In view of the shortage of paper, what about crossing these birds with cockatoos and teaching them to deliver verbal messages.'

Early in the war, according to an excellent book called *Birds and the War* by Hugh S. Gladstone, parrots were employed by the French on the Eiffel Tower, to announce the approach of hostile aircraft. It was found that the birds gave warning of aeroplanes or airships twenty minutes before they arrived. The parrots, however, unlike the horses at the front (see Goodbye, Old Man), could never discriminate between German and Allied planes, and the scheme was scrapped.

Many lives were also saved towards the end of the war by pigeons homing from sea planes in distress. At first the pilots were very sceptical, and roared with derisive laughter at the thought of having to take pigeons along as passengers. After the following story appeared in the *Daily Mail* on 1 January 1918, however, they hastily changed their minds. A seaplane patrolling the North Sea was forced down, and in danger of being smashed to pieces by heavy seas. One of the airmen managed to release the pigeon, with a message asking for help. It homed 22 miles in 22 minutes. Help arrived and saved all the crew, who were clinging to a plane that was just about to break up.

Another small pigeon died bringing news of a badly damaged plane. All the crew were picked up from the sea but one can imagine how they felt later when they discovered that their gallant saviour had died in the attempt. They had him mounted in a glass case and put in the mess with the inscription, 'A very gallant gentleman'.

Some pigeons met a less glorious end. The *Daily Mail* ran a story in 1919 that, when hard pressed to find dinner for his master, a faithful batman served up what he described as a brace of birds. They were remarkably tasty but a subsequent enquiry from headquarters as to the loss of two valuable homing pigeons led to investigation. The batman at last revealed the origins of dinner to his master, and after being warned that this could mean a court martial, and had he left any evidence as to the basket, replied that he couldn't cook the pigeons without a fire.

Pigeons in both wars were dropped with spies, and were sent home when there was anything important to report. As a result of this the poor pigeon was ludicrously libelled during the war, no spy play or novel being complete without one or two pigeons, invariably working for the Germans. Everyone knew of the story of the marketwoman whose bosom flew away when she was arrested. Pigeons were also involved in counterespionage. The metal German message-carrier, which was far more elaborate than the English model, was brilliantly copied by a craftsman in Birmingham, and soon pigeons wearing it were being flown into Germany with dud messages.

When they first invaded France, the Germans issued a hefty fifty franc fine to anyone keeping pigeons, and many unfortunate fanciers were forced to destroy their birds. Many escaped however and fled to the country, where they were shot at by starving German soldiers, or even more sadly stoned if they took refuge on some peasant's roof, because civilians were so terrified of incurring fines.

One of the most poignant and heartbreaking episodes of the whole war took place on the morning of 8 October 1914, when Commander Denuit, the head of the Belgian Pigeon Service, took a flaming torch to the Great Colombier in Antwerp and, tears streaming down his face, burnt alive 2,500 of the finest pigeons in the world, rather than let them fall into the hands of the Germans. One can only appreciate what this sacrifice cost him if one realises that pigeon fanciers grow as fond of their birds as we might of a dog or a cat. The brave Commander was only just in time; the Germans captured Antwerp at noon.

On the home front in March 1918, when people were invited to invest their money in war bonds, a pigeon post service carried messages from the investor's house to the bank in Trafalgar Square, noting the amount invested. A pigeon attracted huge crowds when it arrived from Marlborough House with the message that Queen Alexandra wished to purchase

5,000 war savings certificates on behalf of the Queen Alexandra League.

More than 100,000 pigeons served Great Britain in the First World War, and a commendable 95 per cent returned with their messages. Despite this, the pigeon navy, airforce and army were summarily demobbed at the end of the war.

The authorities were convinced that, with the advent of radar, backed up by the wireless, and the telephone, no one would ever need pigeons again. But it was the same old story. Within a few months of the beginning of World War II, British planes were being forced down into the sea, drenching their radios, which left them with no means of telling their aerodrome where on earth they might be. An urgent S.O.S. was therefore sent out for pigeons. Once again the fanciers offered their own services and that of their best racing pigeons, who were soon housed in lofts in every aerodrome. From then on, nearly all British bombers carried pigeons on flights. If the plane had to be ditched in the sea, the pigeon was thrown clear in a waterproof container in which it could survive for half an hour. The crew then got into their dinghy, picked up the pigeon and despatched it to base asking for help.

One of the most famous pigeons was a blue chequered hen called Winkie, to whom the crew of a Beaufort bomber owed their lives in 1942. The plane was forced down in the North Sea. Winkie, thrown loose, managed to escape from her container and, wings clogged with oily water, set off for home. All night the crew grew colder and colder in their little dinghy, knowing how hopelessly slim their chances were.

Fortunately an exhausted oilstained Winkie was making her way towards the coast of Scotland 129 miles away, and just before dawn a telephone call to the operations room at the crew's aerodrome told of her safe arrival. She had been given no message to carry, but at least she had a code number which gave some indication where her crew might be. The aerodrome put two and two together, and the crew were all rescued. A few days later they held a dinner in the

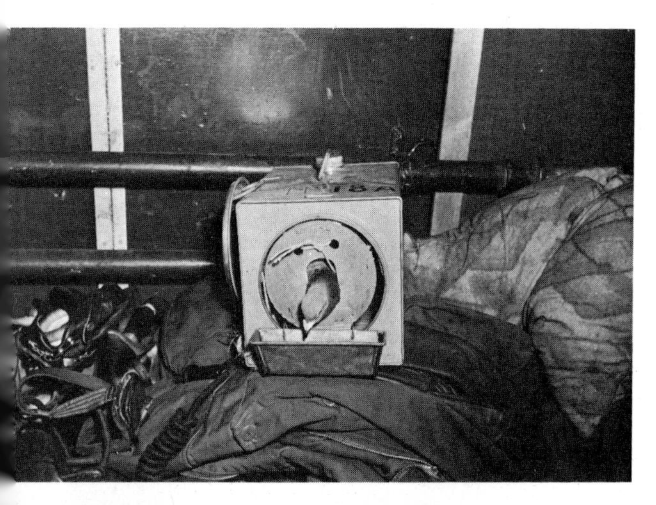

Carrier pigeons were used by aircraft of the RAF Coastal and Bomber Command, and were released with a message in case of emergency. If the aircraft came down into the sea, the pigeon was thrown clear in a container with waterproof lid which clamped down instantly, where it could live for half an hour. When the crew had taken to their dinghy, they picked up the pigeon container and sent a message to base giving their position. Thus the birds saved a number of lives. IWM

G.I. Joe, the American pigeon who saved 100 lives in Italy, being admired by crowds at the Tower of London whither he flew (assisted) in 1946 to receive his Dickin Medal. IWM

little pigeon's honour, with Winkie, preening herself in her cage at the end of the table being toasted by admiring officers.

In World War II, pigeons also did valiant work at the front. G.I. Joe, for example, who served with the U.S. forces in Italy, was the first winner of the Dickin Medal who wasn't English.

'On the morning of October 18, 1943,' wrote Dorothea St Hill Bourne in *They Also Serve*, 'a message came from the British 56th (London) Infantry division asking for air support to help break the heavily fortified German position at Colvi Vecchia. It was accordingly arranged that Allied XII Air Support Command should bomb the town. Just as the planes were about to take off, G.I. Joe arrived with a message to say that the 169th Infantry Brigade had captured the village. Five minutes later it would have been too late to stop the bombers. Thus by his rapid flight – 20 miles in the same number of minutes – the American pigeon prevented what might have been a tragedy involving the lives of at least 100 Allied soldiers.'

Winkie, one of the bravest pigeons of World War II, won a Dickin Medal and attended a celebration dinner in her honour given by the crew she saved.

As a reward, in 1946, Joe was flown in luxury from New Jersey and, mindful of the rationing, brought his own bag of pigeon food. Arriving in England, a U.S. Embassy car took him to the Tower of London, where he was met by a distinguished deputation including the constable of the Tower, who was a field marshall, the U.S. Military Attache, several Beefeaters, the Tower ravens, and sundry tower cats with watering mouths. A speech was then made by a British Major-General, in which he congratulated Joe personally, before hanging his medal round his neck.

In World War I, pigeons who were wounded in active service were promptly pensioned off, became the pets of the aerodrome, and were given names like Haigh and Kitchener. In World War II life was rougher and it was back to work as soon as they'd recovered. One of the bravest pigeons, and another Dickin Medal winner; was Mary of Exeter, who flew from 1940 until the end of the war by which time she had had twenty-two stitches in her little body. Once she vanished for nearly a week, but finally arrived with her message, with her neck and right breast ripped open, having been attacked by a hawk. Two months

Pigeon Mary of Exeter was presented with the Dickin Medal (no. 32) by Sir James Ross of the Air Ministry, on 29 November 1945. She served from 1940 until the end of the war and was badly wounded by a hawk; on another occasion she had part of her wing shot away and three pellets in her body. She escaped twice while other pigeons in her loft were killed by German bombs, and on a fifth occasion was picked up more dead than alive from wounds. The wounds she received on three occasions needed a total of 22 stitches. IWM

later, after being lost for three weeks, she fluttered in with one wing shot away, and three pellets in her body. During the German raids on Exeter a large bomb fell outside her loft, killing many of her pigeon friends. This upset her very much, but after a short break she was back at work again, but within ten days was picked up in a field more dead than alive. Thin as a skeleton, she had a huge gash in her head, and more wounds in her body. Her owner nursed her back to health, and as it was difficult for her to hold up her head, she wore a leather collar for some time, until the wound healed.

By the end of the war nearly 200,000 pigeons had been given to the war effort by private fanciers – almost twice as many as in World War I. People tend to dismiss the pigeon's achievement and to say they all just followed a natural instinct to get home as fast as possible. But there are courageous pigeons who battle on, and others who dally by the way. Wing Commander Lea Rayner, who organised the R.A.F. pigeon service at the Air Ministry admitted that once when he had to send a crucial message, he chose two hen pigeons, then introduced them separately to the same very glamorous male pigeon. Before mating could take place, both hens were sent off on their mission. Both hurtled back to the handsome cock pigeon in record time, with only a few minutes between their arrivals. In the same way, one supposes, a man who was married to Bo Derek wouldn't dally in the pub on the way home from work. When pigeons flew at night, large red lights were put outside the lofts to guide them – like many a human counterpart.

Perhaps the most lonely and heroic task performed by pigeons was to be dropped in baskets by parachute into occupied territory in the forlorn hope they might be discovered by a member of the resistance, and sent home with vital information. Several pigeons were lucky enough to find their way back, and tell us the location of German launching sites. This enabled the R.A.F. to bomb these sites and saved many Londoners from the onslaught of flying bombs and rockets. The Nazis, well aware of the value of the messages they were carrying, gunned down thousands of pigeons. Vicious hawks were also kept in the Pas de Calais area to tear these small messengers to pieces. Probably one of them got Mary of Exeter.

During the last three and a half years of the war, 16,544 pigeons were parachuted into occupied countries. The stark fact is that only 1,842 (or less than one in eight) returned. What this meant to their owners, who had lent them so nobly to the war effort, can only be appreciated by other pigeon fanciers. Most of them had spent a life time building up a family or a special racing strain and, as has been pointed out before, these men were devoted to their birds. An old lady would have felt the same if she'd had to let her pet mongrel be dropped in a basket into a strange land, knowing that it might be badly hurt in the fall, and in most cases would starve to death before it was ever discovered. Many pigeons were also found by the Germans, or by civilians too frightened to send back information or even open the basket, because of the increasing severity of the German fines.

On a happier note, pigeons were also kept busy serving in the Home Guard, preparing for a possible invasion. One private, on an exercise at Andover, was ordered to send two pigeons with an urgent message to Salisbury. A touch of Dad's Army sets in when he only reached Salisbury bicycling furiously three and a half hours later. Asked by his irate commanding officer what the hell had happened to the message, he replied that he was so worried that the pigeons might get lost on the way he thought he'd better bring them and their messages himself.

Apart from their operational functions, pigeons were useful in other respects. Officers who couldn't get a leave pass often used to borrow a crate of the birds, to release for a training flight from their home town or wherever else in the U.K. they wanted to spend their weekend – this subterfuge counting as a duty. One officer also told me that the pigeon parachutes, suitably cut down and dyed, made excellent evening skirts. His wife evidently had one which was the envy of all her friends.

Other birds besides pigeons served in the two wars. Falcons were trained to keep the airstrips cleared of

The P.D.S.A. Allied Forces Mascot Club: Mrs Dickin OBE presents the Dickin Medal to Winkie of the RAF Pigeon Service. Winkie saved one aircrew by a flight in exceptionally difficult circumstances, and was the first Dickin recipient. She fell into an oil-covered sea, struggled free, and flew 120 miles to her base. With her is Wing Commander Raynor CBE.

Soldier with a cage of canaries 'liberated' from a ruined house in St. Venant, 15 April 1918. IWM

smaller birds, and British submarines in World War II released large amounts of bread. Floating on the top of the sea it attracted large flocks of sea gulls, and soon gulls were appearing at the sight of any long dark shadow moving under the surface. Their wheelings and screamings were observed by people along the shore, the place noted, and if it didn't tie up with the known position of a friendly submarine the appropriate British countermeasures would be taken. More frivolous attempts were made by naval intelligence to train sea gulls to obscure German periscopes with their droppings.

Mention also must be made of the little canaries, who served so bravely in the first war. Fifteen times more sensitive than humans to gas, canaries, mice and sometimes even cats were widely used both by our own and German miners at the front when tunnelling, to detect the presence of gas. 'Many was the night,' wrote a sorrowing soldier about a dead canary, 'when he was rudely disturbed from his slumber, dumped unceremoniously in a bag, and carried through rain and snow up to the trenches.'

Sisters on a British ambulance train near Doullens, 27 April 1918, with the caged canaries they kept on the train. These were allegedly to cheer the wounded, but possibly intended to give early warning of gas attacks.

At the end of World War II, the pigeon service was of course disbanded. But in America many attempts have since been made to train suicide pigeons to ride inside missiles and direct them towards aircraft carriers, destroyers and radar stations. If the missiles were guided, the pigeon's job was to peck at its seed which in turn pressed a battery which directed the missile on a random course to fox the enemy, although eventually it reached its target.

Behavioural scientists in America also tried to train pigeons to detect ambushes in the Vietnam War. They were taught to peck their seed whenever the image of a man appeared on a screen. Robert Lubow, in *The War Animals*, describes how they were trained to pick out all kinds of human figures, 'lying down, standing up, black, white and yellow, semi-nude and nude', but doesn't tell us how the pigeons reacted to monkeys. The scientists hoped to raise half a million dollars to research the project further. But, alas, the crucial test to assess their military usefulness had to be cancelled indefinitely because all the pigeons caught pigeon pox!

The Camel

Can't! Don't! Shan't! Won't!
Pass it along the line!
Somebody's pack has slid from his back,
Wish it were only mine!
Somebody's load has tipped off in the road—
Cheer for a halt and a row!
Urrgh! Yarrh! Grr! Arrh!
Somebody's catching it now.

RUDYARD KIPLING: *Commissariat Camels*

It might appear that the average soldier spent more time fighting his camel than the enemy. But the poor beast can be excused his cantankerousness, when one considers how dreadfully he has suffered over the centuries, because of the ignorance of the men who forced him into battle. In the desert, the camel has the edge over the horse and the mule. He can carry heavy loads for long distances without food or water. For this task, he is equipped with a hump that acts as a kind of petrol tank and with long, sheltering eyelashes, heavy eyelids, and slit nostrils which close right up in a sandstorm. What none of the great military leaders ever appreciated was that he cannot cope with temperatures below zero.

When the Russians were campaigning in Central Asia, a force under General Skobeloff set out with 12,000 splendid transport camels. The stark, horrifying truth is that he returned a few months later with only one camel. In the Afghan campaign, the British lost 30,000 camels largely because they had no idea how to look after them. Unable to cope with the snow and icy rain, camels died like flies in the harsh winters of the Crimean War. During the siege of Sebastapol, the poor camel mascot of the Royal Engineers was found frozen to death on Christmas Eve.

Camels also took part in the Gordon Relief Campaign in Egypt, and died once again in their thousands from exhaustion and starvation. During the shilly-shallying as to whether Gordon should be rescued, Sir Garnett Wolseley, the British Commander-in-Chief who was based at Korti in the Sudan, decided to form a camel corps to act as a mounted infantry. Its function would be to take a short cut across the Bayudu desert to warn the Mahdi's supporters that the British meant business, and if necessary it would push on to Khartoum to save Gordon.

Known as the Nile Circus, the Camel Corps's exploits are beautifully described by Lord Anglesey in the third volume of his magnificent *History of the British Cavalry*. The Circus consisted of four camel regiments, comprising some 1,789 officers and men, drawn from the cavalry and the guards, who found it very infra dig to have to exchange their splendid horses for these strange, refractory beasts.

Ship of the Crimea: a seaman mounted on a camel on his way to Balaklava – but not wearing one! IWM

Camels provided vital transport during the Second Afghan War. They are shown here at Fort Jumwood in 1879. LC

With a classic example of the blind leading the blind, two rough-riding sergeants, one of whom had never seen a camel before, were sent out from England to teach the new Corps how to ride. Eight thousand camels costing on an average £13 each were purchased, although Captain Lord Charles Beresford R.N. paid £24 for his famous racing camel Bimbashi. The best camels came from Arabia.

'The pace is so smooth,' wrote Lieutenant Count Gleichen of the Grenadier Guards, 'that the test at the Mecca Tattersalls is for the rider to carry a full cup of coffee, if he spills any, the camel is considered underbred.'

A camel may be a comfortable ride, but he is not easy to control. When one is perched on his hump, his neck descends and rises again like the Khyber Pass, and his head swings as wildly as a jib in a high wind. Lord Cochrane found the Corps's first attempts at riding very funny. He observed two or three camels running away with their riders, who were hanging on with one leg, with their heads hanging underneath the camels' bellies. Later when Sir Garnett Wolseley inspected the Corps, ten men fell off.

Camels were also a nuisance in the lines. They caught colds easily; and they were picky drinkers, often hanging about for quarter of an hour, then refusing to drink at all if jostled. They were always getting caught in their ropes, or breaking them and wandering malevolently off to cause trouble in the horse lines. Their redeeming feature was that they were calm under fire. In 1722, the Afghans invented a cannon light enough to be fired from the back of a sitting camel, and in Korti a square of camels didn't flinch when blanks and shells were fired at them and over them. Even when they were charged by the 19th Hussars, yelling and cheering, only one camel scram-

Camel Transport Corps: a line of camels picketed in Palestine in the summer of 1918. IWM

bled to its feet, then feeling rather foolish sat down again.

In December 1884, the Camel Corps set off across the desert towards Khartoum, with 2,195 camels carrying the supplies. Within eleven days, the poor beasts were breaking down in all directions, with sores full of maggots and big enough to put your fist in. Lord Anglesey quotes an officer in the 5th Lancers, who noticed 'the camel went slower and slower, until the tail of the animal in front, to which he was attached, looked like dropping off, then he would stop for a second, give an almighty shiver and drop down dead.'

Lord Charles Beresford, obviously a kind man who liked animals, found that, like tired hunters, camels that were off their food could be tempted if they were fed in tiny handfuls. Later he had the unenviable task of ordering fallen camels to be lifted to their feed with a gun pole, so men could be loaded onto them. This would get another thirty or forty miles out of the wretched animals until they finally collapsed never to rise again.

In World War II, camels were also sacrificed in their thousands to aid the essential transport in Eritrea and Somaliland, and the small Somaliland Camel Corps heroically kept at bay an Italian invading force of twenty-six battalions of artillery and tanks, until reinforcements arrived. Vast numbers of shaggy brown Tibetan camels were also used by the Russian armies.

The camel's finest hour, however, occurred earlier in the First World War, when in order to drive the Turks out of the desert, General Allenby employed the largest, best organised camel force the world has ever known. According to E.H. Baynes, in *Animal Heroes of the Great War*, if you rode your horse back along the double convoy of camels, you could keep going for forty miles.

The camel carried food, medical supplies and ammunition, but his most vital role was to have two water tanks lashed to his pack saddle, and to keep pace with the troops in the field.

'I have vivid recollections,' writes Geoffrey Inchbald in his excellent book *Imperial Camel Corps*, 'after the capture of Beersheba, when the forward troops ran out of water, and we lay all day under a burning sun without a drop to drink, and without any hope of one, until a large convoy of camels arrived carrying sufficient for the needs of something like three divisions.'

One of the greatest headaches was recruiting camels for this vast force. The task inevitably fell on the A.V.C. who travelled all over the Middle East, buying them in from Egypt, Somaliland, India and the Sudan. This presented further problems; the camel is a creature of caprice, who may chew the cud calmly in the firing line, but will suddenly take fright at the flapping of a tent or the bray of a donkey.

E.H. Baynes's account of 200 camels arriving in Cairo is like an Ealing comedy. Something suddenly upset them, and they bolted, straight through a nearby British camp. Some charged into tents, waking the sleeping soldiers who thought the enemy had arrived. Others tripped over guy ropes, and crashed grumbling furiously to the ground. Three officers retreated into a tent which was suddenly invaded by two evil-looking beasts poking their heads through the door, and trying to grab them with long yellow teeth. Fortunately the tent collapsed, temporarily blindfold-

Indian camel transport crossing the River Tigris. IWM

Camel washing at the water's edge. IWM

ing the camels so the officers were able to escape. One Major, formerly the superintendent of the Cairo Fire Brigade, spent a hazardous hour in a signal box besieged by furious camels.

The camel's constitution caused even more concern than his temperament. For despite his refractory nature, he was a delicate animal even when living in hot climates. If his food were left on the ground, he was so greedy that he licked up grains of sand as well, which gave him colic, which in turn led to fatal ulcers of the stomach. All the camels caught mange, and the few members of the A.V.C. who were not out recruiting more camels worked from dawn to midnight trying to keep this particularly virulent complaint in check.

Most of the animals arrived with nothing but a head collar, and the A.V.C. was then faced with the even more monumental problem of finding 50,000 pack saddles. A camel may start off on a trek in marvellous condition with a large hump and well-rounded sides, but after a few week's campaigning with little forage and less water, his body shrinks beyond belief, and the saddle that once fitted him causes him terrible sores. Many attempts were made to find a suitable saddle, and in the end one was produced from wood and canvas, with girths of webbing, which adjusted to the ups and downs of the camel's figure rather like stretch jeans.

As has already been pointed out, camels are tricky to water; even after a march of several days they would refuse to touch brackish water. They couldn't be allowed to drink from lakes or rivers because they got

Camel Transport Corps in Palestine. A line of stock camels picketing; they had been selected for breeding purposes in Egypt. IWM

their feet wet, which led to foot trouble. Nor could any camel be taken from the trough until all the other animals had drunk, because they are such herd animals that the slow drinker would tend to leave with his companions before he had had enough. Moreover, when a camel drank deeply he spread enormously in size, so one had the ludicrous situation of the camels in the middle swelling out like pumpkins, until the ones on the outside were pushed away from the trough.

Once they were in the field, the problems multiplied. Camels usually tolerated the men who rode and looked after them, but this didn't stop them suddenly swinging round and biting kneecaps off or bringing their hind legs round in a vicious semicircular kick. Male camels also became completely ungovernable in the mating season, when they went off their food, developed appalling bad breath, and rushed round with a pink bladder (actually an extension of their palates) frothing out of the side of their mouths like bubble gum. If unmuzzled, they would charge any man and carry him off, like a big dog might savage a rag doll. There is a horrible story, after one male camel went beserk, of a booted left leg being discovered in the sand – minus its owner. The camels' fangs were also long and very dirty, so a bite often led to blood poisoning, particularly when other camels were attacked. If muzzled, a camel was quite capable of knocking a man over and kneeling on him, until all the breath was driven out of his body.

Camels are divided into two species. The first, known as the Bactrian camel, has two humps and a thick coat which grows long in winter and enables him to withstand near Siberian conditions.

The second species is the one-humped Arabian

camel, generally called a dromedary (they, to complicate matters, often come from Bactria). A dromedary can keep going for 25–30 miles a day for weeks on end, with a load of 450 lbs including his rider. Dromedaries were used in Allenby's desert campaign. Unfortunately, unlike the Bactrian camels, they can't stand extreme cold. As a result they suffered appalling hardships in the winter of 1917–18 when Allenby was marching on Jerusalem and Amman.

'There was nothing more pathetic than the camels,' wrote Geoffrey Inchbald.

Most of them weren't unsaddled for days. On 6th December after the surrender of Jerusalem, they were so weak, they couldn't stand up. In many cases, they had cavities on each side of their humps, so deep you could have buried a cricket ball in them. The cavities went septic, and the raw flesh was alive with maggots. God only knows what these once splendid animals must have suffered, but they complained no more than usual and stuck it out until they collapsed from exhaustion. Looking back along the route we had passed, we could see an endless line of corpses fading into the distance.

It was bad enough in the Palestine plains, where the camels sank into the mud up to their girths, and had to be abandoned, but the most pathetic thing was when these sand-orientated creatures were asked to climb up the rocky Judean hills, loaded with supplies because no truck or lorry could cross such difficult territory. One can hardly bear to imagine the poor camels, their long, gangling, spindly legs struggling for footholds, sharp stones cutting their delicate feet at every stride, with icy rain pouring down making the tracks slippery. Frequently camels did the splits never to rise again; others broke legs or were so overloaded they lost their balance and pitched terrified into the crevasses, from which there was no hope of retrieving them. There were few spare camels, except the wounded, so when one collapsed, his load was divided among the remaining beasts who struggled heroically on.

The Turkish enemy was also fully aware of the importance of the supplies the camels were bringing up, and bombed the convoys heavily by day. Most of the travelling therefore had to be done by night with the camels being dragged, pushed, and even lifted bodily by the men up and down the steepest mountains.

'An Australian with his wrist in a camel's mouth.' Taken near Shellal, 17 September 1917. IWM

There were, thank goodness, lighter moments during the desert campaign. General Chauvel, Commander-in-Chief of the Australian Light Horse, wrote home on 17 September 1917, describing the camel brigades' sports at El Arish.

I have never seen anything so funny as musical chairs on camels, the men had to ride bareback round a big ring, while the music was playing. When it stopped they dismounted and led their camels up to the sandbags. As a camel dislikes being hurried beyond all things, and objects to going out for a walk when he is being led, it was not always the smartest men who got the chairs. You never saw anything so ridiculous as the camels keeping time to the music, and one of them started waltzing in the middle of the ring.

Towards the end of the war, when the supply of

Camel of Transport Corps and foal – or Accidents Will Happen. IWM

camels ran out, the authorities took the extreme step of signing up 3,000 cow camels, most of whom, though of a refreshingly gentle nature, were pregnant. This caused chaos, as they all gave birth on the march. The animal-besotted British soldier was of course very taken by these blond silken-furred helpless little creatures (who looked like 'anthills on sticks') and refused to leave them behind. As a result the babies were folded up like picnic tables, placed in camel nets, and slung on one side of their mothers' pack saddles. In this way, they travelled for six hours, then were let down for a drink and a scamper.

Apart from the 50,000 transport camels, there were also several regiments mounted on camels. The most glamorous of these was certainly the Imperial Camel Corps which was made up almost entirely of contingents from British Yeomanry, and Australian and New Zealand regiments. Together they took part in the attack on Beersheba, the advance on Philistian, and the Amman and Es Salt raids, and when working with T.E. Lawrence's troop of Arab riders, they seriously harrassed the Turk in their attempts to get to Damascus.

The Imperial Camel Corps was also a valuable asset to the mounted troops during operations in the desert. For unlike the horses, the camels suffered no hardship if they went for three or four days without water, and thus as a self-contained fighting force the Corps could reconnoitre and patrol literally thousands of square miles of waterless desert.

When the Corps was founded in 1916, the British Battalion, who were largely ex-cavalry officers, found the camels very comfortable to ride: 'you just put your feet forward over the camel's hump, as though you were sitting in a deck chair.'

T.E. Lawrence, however, coming across the Corps in the desert wrote of 'the laughing, sunburnt khaki-clad men of the Imperial Camel Corps,' and went on to describe how diversely they rode: 'Some sat naturally despite the clumsy saddles, some pushed out their hinderparts and leaned forward like Arab villagers, other lounged in the saddle as if they were Australians riding horses.'

The Camel Corps had some exciting scraps in the desert with the enemy. One day, while out on patrol,

Indian despatch riders at Kut-el-Amara, though quite where they are going and why is not clear. IWM

The Imperial Camel Corps Brigade marching into Beersheba on 17 November 1917. IWM

they came across a Turkish ammunition and baggage column. A third of the corps were ordered to dismount and give covering fire, the rest charged in extended formation, yelling their heads off, and firing their rifles from the saddle. Needless to say, they didn't hit anything, but the Turks were so astounded, they only put up the slightest resistance, and 68 Turks and 14 valuable baggage mules were taken prisoner. The Camel Corps's casualties were only two men slightly hurt, and seven camels hit.

Camels were incredibly stoical. Just as they struggled gamely on in the Judean hills until they dropped, they would endure pain and, unless mortally wounded, would carry on as before. The slightly wounded ones showed no surprise or concern even when blood was pouring out of their noses.

Geoffrey Inchbald denies that all camels were wild and savage, saying that it entirely depended on how they were treated. He had one favourite camel, who was a most gentle amenable creature: 'We became very attached to one another, which was just as well since he carried me for well over 2,000 miles. Our lives were in their humps and we thought a lot of them.'

It was also possible to outwit a camel. Normally he

refused to enter a railway truck, but if you blindfolded him, turned him round until he was dizzy, backed him up to the ramp, and then pulled like mad in the other direction, out of sheer bloody-mindedness he would immediately back up into the truck and be furious after the blindfold was removed that he'd been fooled.

Despite the plagues of flies, the temperatures of 120° in the shade, and most of the men catching mange from the camels which caused them to itch terribly all night, the Imperial Camel Corps seemed to get a lot of fun out of their mounts. They discovered for example that the camel will eat anything. One day according to Geoffrey Inchbald, one camel consumed three tins of salmon, tin included, and several boxes of matches without any ill effects. On another hilarious occasion, the authorities wanted to see what effects a gas attack would have on camels. Because they were really fond of their animals, the Corps selected as a guinea pig one very sick camel, who hadn't eaten for days and who was far too weak to stand up.

The gas men released their gas, and the next moment the poor invalid disappeared in a cloud of noxious substance, which didn't disperse for some minutes, when to the delight of the men, the camel was seen to be standing up, grazing happily. She'd proved more than a match for the Chlorine.

Europe: 'You gotta get up, you gotta get up. . .' Taken near Gera in Germany, the camel 'acquired' by the American soldier from a 'caravan', was taking groups of Germans and Poles from Chemnitz to the Rheinland.

The Mule

Last came the screw guns, and Billy the mule carried himself as though he commanded all the troops, and his harness was oiled and polished till it winked. I gave a cheer all by myself for Billy the mule, but he never looked right or left.

RUDYARD KIPLING: *The Jungle Book*

The mule has often had a bad press. The symbol of obstinacy, cantankerous, cussed, he has neither the highly-strung beauty of his mother, the horse, nor the endearing fluffiness of his father, the donkey. He has no aptitude for galloping or jumping, so he was spurned by the cavalry and the artillery. Yet anyone who served with him was a convert for life. For like most mongrels, the mule is highly intelligent, bursting with character, and full of heart.

Mr R.J. Cox, an ex-cavalry officer writing in the *British Mule Society Magazine*, confesses that when he was first put in charge of mules in World War II, he felt he had fallen right off the social ladder. It was only through working with these deeply idiosyncratic beasts that he came to respect and love them: 'Having had experience of mules, donkeys and horses, I would always choose a mule . . . I might not make a showy start, but I should still be going after everyone had stopped.'

Although the Indian Army has consistently used mules in the mountains, the British Army, as might be expected, was extremely slow to latch on to their great possibilities. In 1912, they bought one mule from America. It was such a wild success that in 1913 they bought three. It took a crisis like World War I for them to appreciate the mule's sterling virtues, and by the end of the hostilities 40,000 had been bought from America. So great in fact was the mule's impact that in World War II he totally ousted the horse from the centre of the stage.

It is this mongrel quality of being half horse, half donkey, known as hybrid vigour, that gives mules their amazing stamina. They endured the terrible conditions of the trenches at Vimy Ridge, for example, far better than the horse. Horses dropped like flies, but not one mule died, nor even fell sick. Three quarters of the ammunition at Passchendaele was delivered by mules. Hundreds drowned in the cavernous shell holes, but here again, even on reduced rations, they didn't fall sick, and were incredibly brave under fire. Mules also coped stoically with the heat at Gallipolli and with the bitter cold of the Balkans, where they were often found in the morning with frost silvering their ears, and a rug of snow on their backs.

Pack mules taking ammunition in wicker carriers up to Pilckem Ridge during the Battle of Ypres, 16 August 1917. IWM

Having withstood the elements and the enemy, however, mules weren't so enthusiastic about their own side. One day in France when a man came out of the lines, leading a mule and wearing one of the first gas masks, all the mules broke their ropes and ran away. It took two men, without gas masks, two days to round them up.

By the end of the war, however, the mules' excellent health record had won approval all round. Only one mule compared with four horses, for example, suffered from mange. One mule for every four and a half horses became severely debilitated. One mule – who would eat anything from head collars to another mule's tail – for every eight horses suffered from indigestion. About equal numbers went lame, and if a mule contracted bone lameness, he seldom recovered. But on the credit side, he was a much better passenger than the horse. Deeply suspicious of trains, trucks and transports, he often baulked on embarking; but once aboard, he settled in philosophically, and twice as many horses as mules died or were injured in transit.

Admittedly, a mule could be a tricky customer. He

World War I: this poor mule, badly wounded on the Italian front, is comforted by veterinary staff. IWM

German East African campaign, 1914-18. During the heavy rains animals, cars, and heavy vehicles were taken across the river by cable. Ruwu River, near Ruwu Tp, April 1917. IWM

had a terrible cow kick, and could kill a dog with one crack of his hoof. He has been described as the only animal who can mount himself. But as M.D. Daunt points out in his marvellous essay *In Praise of Mules*, it is a case of one bad apple. Of the 200 mules Mr Daunt supervised, only one was really dangerous; and he was a killer. If you took your eyes off him for a second, he had you in his teeth, shaking you like a terrier with a rat. There always had to be two men in the stable with him, one to groom, one to watch. Another of his tricks was to get a man on the ground and crush the life out of him. The problem in both World Wars was that many men met mules for the first time, and many mules had their first encounters with partially trained drivers, with disastrous consequences. Mules respond to amateurs with their teeth and their heels. But with an expert and kindly driver, and liberal supplies of sugar, the most difficult mules become biddable.

Like many husbands, in fact, you cannot coerce the mule, but he will do anything if he thinks it's his idea in the first place. This is probably why he is most successful as a mountain pack animal. In France, mules tended to be part of a team pulling a gun. But you can't drag a big gun through a Burmese jungle or up a steep winding mountain track in India, so you divided it up into six, and each of half a dozen mules carried one of the gun parts on his pack saddle. When needed, a good gun team reckoned they could whip the separate parts off the mules, assemble one of these 'screw guns' and be ready for action in a minute.

The mule was in his element in such situations. He never slipped on those steep winding tracks; he never panicked; and as long as he was able to select his own route up a hill, he didn't mind pulling the driver up hanging on his tail. Kipling put it perfectly:

As me and my companions were scrambling up a hill,
The path was lost in rolling stones, but we went forward still;
For we can wriggle and climb, my lads, and turn up everywhere,
And it's our delight on a mountain height with a leg or two to spare.
Good luck to every sergeant then, that lets us pick our road.
Bad luck to all the driver men that cannot pack a load:
For we can wriggle and climb, etc.

A mule-borne 3.7-inch Howitzer, 1943. IWM

Scraping mud from a mule, near Bernafay Wood on the Somme, November 1916. IWM

If you didn't give him the time to be cussed, the mule could occasionally be outsmarted. Punjabi Muleteers for example were very skilful at loading mules into railway trucks. At the first sign of baulking, the men linked hands together under the mule's hindquarters, as many as possible, like a lacrosse stick, then threw him in.

Mules also had a gift for getting themselves out of trouble. Brigadier A.H. Munn wrote in the *British Mule Society Magazine* of marching in the Simla hills when a mule was pushed over the edge of a precipice and rolled some fifty feet, landing with a thump in the road. Fortunately he tucked his legs in, didn't struggle, and suffered only a few grazes, which didn't stop him marching with his load next day. Any horse to whom the same thing had happened would have panicked and broken his legs.

On one occasion according to Mr Daunt, a lot of battery mules got entangled in some coils of barbed wire. Horses, again, would have gone beserk; but the mules stood still, examined the wire, and extracted themselves without a scratch, 'then ran on with that glorious, gambolling extended trot, ears pricked, head swinging from side to side, and tail swishing in that way mules and horses do when they are free, and know they ought not to be.'

A mule team and limber in difficulties in a muddy area near Potijze Farm, October 1917. IWM

In the Second World War, the mule did not have much fun, but once again, as in the First World War, he died as a result of enemy fire rather than exhaustion or sickness. In January 1940, about 3,000 mules were brought from Cyprus and India to serve in Flanders and France. According to Brigadier J. Clabby in his *History of the Royal Army Veterinary Corps*, during the assault on the Hitler Line the mules were very naughty and kept escaping during operations, braying noisily. On investigation, the R.A.V.C. found that the mules were much above themselves, through too much food and too little work.

The soldiers had to learn that mules were not vicious, merely mischievous. They were to cut down the rations, and put them to work. In time, the most troublesome mules invariably turned out to be the bravest and most hardworking; and all through the coldest winter for years in France, they carried ammunition and supplies up to the forward positions. No suitable shoes were available, and the poor animals slipped all over the icy roads.

Feeding an exhausted mule on the road somewhere on the Western Front. IWM

Later, one Indian Mule Company was captured in the Blitzkreig of May 1940. But the other animal units managed to withdraw to Dunkirk. Tragically, there was only room on the boats for the soldiers to escape, so the poor mules were abandoned to the enemy, which must have broken many a returning driver's heart.

For the rest of the war, mules were employed in Tunisia and Eritrea, and 20,000 served in the Hellenic campaign. Some of the mules destined for Greece never got there. On 23 April 1941, the *Santa Clara Valley*, a transport carrying five hundred mules, was divebombed and sunk in shallow waters. Despite repeated bombing, gallant attempts were made by the Veterinary Officer, Captain R.A. Macrae, to put the animals from the upper deck overboard, so they could swim ashore to Greece. Nothing, alas, could be done for the mules trapped below. Later several mules which had swum ashore were found helpless and exhausted on the rocks under a high cliff, and had to be shot. The mules that did reach Greece however, endeared themselves to the Greek officers, many of whom told the R.S.P.C.A. that their only ambition after the war was to drive around the country in a cart drawn by these rather wayward creatures.

When the Allies landed in Italy on 10 July 1943, narrow beaches soon gave way to mountains. By the time Mount Etna (10,741 feet) was reached, the Allies suddenly decided they needed some mules. In December, therefore, the desperately overworked remount department, now under the aegis of the R.A.V.C., was ordered to find 13,000 mules for pack and mounted battery work. The usual shambles ensued. Mules were shipped in, enlisted locally or marched across country. Many of them arrived in only a head collar, so many got hurt on the journey by truck or bit through the ropes and ran away. There was also a desperate shortage of veterinary supplies and rugs. Shoes had to be wrenched off the feet of dead mules,

The stiffest opposition met by the Eighth Army in its drive northwards in Italy was from extensive demolitions. Mules were used where roads were too damaged to take any other form of transport. These mules are equipped with special harnesses to take wounded back from forward areas on stretchers and saddle chairs. IWM

Monte Camino, Italy, 1944. A string of pack mules being led by men of the newly formed mule company through the ruins of San Clemente, a small village. IWM

and hammered on to the feet of the unfortunate live ones by barely trained, terrified Sicilian farriers. Saddles were even more urgently needed than shoes; a dead mule was only disaster if he floated out to sea with his pack saddle on. Soon the mules were wading through mud up to their bellies, bringing ammunition to the tanks bogged down at Monte Camino. Their winter coats became encrusted with mud like cement. Conditions were worse than in Flanders in the First World War.

One ludicrous situation occurred when remounts from Iran and Persia arrived, which were mostly grey mules. The Americans were alarmed that this colour was too conspicuous, and insisted that the mules be dyed a rejuvenating brown like Grecian 2000. But when winter came, it was decided that grey mules showed up less in the snow, and the mules were allowed to go back to their natural colour.

Sometimes the mules got their own back. There was a chronic shortage of forage, and on one occasion a unit of No. 35 Indian Mule Company moved close to the top of a hill overlooking Orsogna, which was strongly held by the Germans. A Bofors gun was hidden near the summit behind a haystack. When the dawn came, there was no haystack – only an enraged brigade major. No. 35 pack company had passed that way.

In Burma, the Chindits of General Wingate's army and the special forces operating between the Japanese

A mule serving with a Chindit column, Burma 1943, in the process of crossing a river. LC

lines used mules to carry ammunition and supplies. Five hundred horses and 3,000 mules were flown into jungle airstrips, and many more were lifted to General Chiang Kai-Shek's forces in China. This time, a lighter, smaller mule was used, and four flew in a Dakota. Coconut matting was put on the floor, to stop the animals slipping, and only 4 mules out of the 3,000 had to be shot as they broke loose in the air, and threatened to kick the plane out. When there was no airstrip the mules were drugged and dropped by parachute.

Burma, 1943 – 'hitchhiking'. LC

It was found when the first mules arrived that their persistent braying on patrols and in camp was advertising our presence to the Japanese. The only answer, the R.A.V.C. decided, was to silence them. So between 1943 and 1945, 5,563 mules and horses had their vocal cords cut under general anaesthetic. All the mules could produce after this was a pathetic strangulated croak – dumb animals indeed. Fortunately, they did not feel the ill effects for long, and were back to work in a fortnight.

One mule who didn't bear a grudge after such cavalier treatment was Mitzi. Her driver, Douglas Roberts, was a Chindit serving with the special force in the Burma campaign. At night Mitzi always bit through her rope and wandered off into the jungle, but was back at first light to be saddled up. She and Mr Roberts were utterly devoted and got each other out of numerous scrapes. Finally, running from the Japs, they stumbled totally exhausted on the furiously rushing river leading down to the Ledo Road, which no man could cross. As they had so far survived, Mitzi was determined to get them both to safety, and plunged into the water. Somehow Mr Roberts clung on to her tail, and swimming gallantly, she towed him to the other side. Mr Roberts remembers Brigadier 'Mad Mike' Calvert on a grey horse saying 'Well done soldier,' before he was lifted on to a stretcher and taken to a hospital. But as he looked at Mitzi, he saw she was dead, and could have echoed the Brigadier's words by saying 'Well done, Mitzi.'

Mules were not merely indifferent to danger, but incredibly courageous. In parts of Africa where horses are bred in country infested with leopard, half a dozen mules added to the herd will effectively protect the younger foals.

Mr Bean, another gallant mule based at H.Q. of Mountain Battery, had been detailed to carry wire for a signal party laying out a line on the Mayu range early in 1944. The path lay through thick scrub, and was very steep. On their return, the party ran into a platoon of Japanese. The soldiers made themselves scarce, dropping down the hillside, leaving Mr Bean to

A train of pack mules carries supplies, having been flown by Dakota to Myitkyina airstrip where the allied infantry were fighting to liberate the city. Chinese and American troops drove the Japanese out on 4 August 1944, 78 days after the siege began.

The mule is a reluctant flyer – hardly surprising, when he can no longer bray his disapproval. This one is resisting being flown behind the Japanese lines in northern Burma in 1944. IWM face the music. Surprised and pained to be so abandoned, he charged the Japs, kicking up his heels in a show of rage. Later he met up with the rest of the party and, as the Japs were approaching, the battery moved on and marched all night. It was only when Mr Bean was unsaddled next day that his driver was appalled to find a long slit oozing pus. A bullet had pierced and cracked his ribs, and he'd never complained once.

Over and over again, one comes across tales of a fatally wounded mule refusing to drop dead till he has carried his pack home to safety. Brigadier Munn describes the pathetic sight of a driver, sitting down cradling his animal's head in his arms and weeping bitterly. The amazing Punjabi Mussalmen and the Dat Sikhs, who were only paid £1.20 a month in the last war, were so fond of their mules that they refused to take any leave, so appalling was the thought of anyone else looking after their 'long-haired darlings'. In the same way, in the jungle in Burma, the drivers would start cutting grass for their animals immediately after unloading, however long the march. And often the mules returned the affection: an officer in the R.H.A. in the First World War wrote in the *Yorkshire Post* of the mules following their drivers round like big dogs, 'nuzzling them all the time in friendship'.

What endeared the mules so much to the soldiers was that each one was a character. They were also no respecters of rank, and positively enjoyed bringing down the mighty by their seats. There was always a mule, looking as though butter wouldn't melt in his mouth, who could be relied on to take a bite out of the backside of an unpopular inspecting officer as he passed down the lines. But by the time he'd whipped round the old mule would have his head back asleep in the manger.

M.D. Daunt tells the endearing story against himself of one particularly gentle country bred mule, on whom he always allowed the nervous inexperienced recruits to practise. One day a young soldier was making heavy weather of picking out his hind feet.

'No, no,' said Mr Daunt, and showing him how to do it, added, 'You don't even have to hold the hoof with your hands, it just lies on your thigh.'

'At that,' Mr Daunt goes on '150 Mule took his hoof off my thigh, placed it gently against my seat and pushed so that I fell on my face behind him, unhurt, but discomfited. It was a gentle reproof for showing off.'

Nor does the mule suffer fools gladly. After the war one opinionated but comparatively inexperienced R.A.V.C. officer was posted to the Army Mule School in Hong Kong. Knowing nothing about mules, he was worried they'd catch cold, and one mild winter night insisted that they should all be rugged up. In the morning, the only part of the new rugs not eaten were the buckles. Only one mule showed any ill effects. When he was opened up, sure enough, a buckle was found. On another occasion the same officer, not realising the mules' disinclination to jump, thought it would be a novelty to build a little jumping lane. Unfortunately he left the timber to build the jumps in the mules' field. Next morning like beavers, they'd eaten the lot. One can imagine what secret mirth this caused in the rest of the staff.

The Mule School had its share of characters: Jimmy Gray who always led you home when you got lost in the jungle, who was a devil to load into the truck on Monday morning, but who was always first in when the week's work was over on Friday night. Then there was Smoky, a big grey mule, who hated vets, and bit and kicked them in the normal course of events. One day, however, he got a narrow stake through his side and, realising a vet was the only thing that might save his life, behaved like an angel. The minute he was better, he started kicking everyone again.

It seems sad that the military careers of such colourful, individual creatures came to an end when cutbacks closed the Mule School in 1975. There are no mules now in the British army, but they would have been invaluable in the Falklands and would have humped all that equipment over the hills without batting an eyelid. A helicopter is grounded by fog, but the mule soldiers on. The army is the poorer.

The Elephant

We lent to Alexander the strength
of Hercules,
The wisdom of our foreheads, the
cunning of our knees;
We bowed our necks to service –
they ne'er were loosed again –
Make way there way for the
ten-foot teams
Of the Forty-pounder train!

RUDYARD KIPLING: *Parade song of the Camp Animals*

The elephant is the egghead of the animal military league. In the 1942–5 Burma campaign, he worked backbreakingly hard for the Allies, building bridges and roads, and helping to build and launch far more ships for us than ever Helen did for Greece. But it was not just his size and strength that impressed people, but the way he used his brain.

As Field Marshal Sir William Slim pointed out, 'It was the elephant's dignity and intelligence that gained our real respect. To watch an elephant building a bridge, to see the skill with which the great beasts lifted the huge logs, and the accuracy with which they were coaxed into position, was to realise that the elephant was no mere transport animal, but indeed a skilled sapper.'

These words of praise came from the Field Marshal's foreword to *Elephant Bill*, Lt.-Col. J.H. Williams's marvellous book describing how he worked in peace and war with these 'most lovable and sagacious beasts'.

One story from *Elephant Bill* will show not only the extreme intelligence of the elephant but also the touching devotion he felt towards his driver or 'oozie', as he was called in Burma. Colonel Williams and a group of military top brass were once watching elephants building an army bridge. Each elephant had to balance a huge log across his tusks, then hoist it up ten feet onto a raised platform and roll it into place. There was a very real danger that the log might roll backwards and crush the driver perched just behind the elephant's head. After a near miss, one wise animal downed logs, and pondered for a minute. Then he searched round for and found a stout stick and wedged it vertically between one of his tusks and his trunk, so the log was checked if it rolled backwards. Thus assured of his driver's safety, he carried on picking up logs and lifting them onto the platform as easily as a mobile crane.

An elephant hauling timber from forest to woodyard, assisting the Burmese war effort to build ships for the Allies on the banks of the Chindwin River. IWM

It is sad, therefore, that so often in earlier wars, the elephant was employed for his brute strength rather than his brain. Hannibal is the military leader always associated with elephants, but in fact it was the Carthaginian general Pyrrhus who, having built up a huge army of elephants imported from the Atlas mountains, first used them against the Romans when he invaded Italy in 280 BC. At the Battle of Heraclea, Pyrrhus somewhat tardily allowed his infantry to clash with the Romans seven times, before unleashing his elephants. The sight of these vast wrinkled monsters with their flapping ears, fearsome tusks and waggling hoover extension noses was enough to make the most disciplined Roman soldier, let alone horse, flee in panic. By this time, however, Pyrrhus had lost 4,000 soldiers, and commented that a further victory as costly in manpower would spell disaster for his campaign. Hence the expression 'Pyrrhic victory'.

It was some sixty years later that Hannibal set out on his historic trek. His vast army which included 90,000 foot soldiers, 12,000 cavalry but only 37 elephants, marched over the Alps and the Pyrenees in order to attack Italy from the back. Hannibal was evidently given to exhorting his troops to greater endeavour on the tops of mountain passes. The elephants obviously didn't approve of this nor of the cold, as only one is supposed to have survived the journey.

More elephant remounts were subsequently imported by Hannibal, but the Romans were beginning to get their measure. They noticed at the Battle of Metaurus in 207 BC that after the first spectacular charge, the elephants got bored and shambled aimlessly round the battlefield. So five years later at the Battle of Zama, when Hannibal released his elephants, the Romans stood their ground leaving large straight gangways between their ranks, and blowing their horns noisily. Thus diverted, the elephants thundered down the gangways and out the other end doing little damage except to the surrounding countryside. As a result, Hannibal was severely defeated.

The Romans also appreciated that the elephant was liable to get out of hand and become more of a danger to his own side. This was borne out in 190 BC when the Syrians under Antiochus the Great failed to beat the Romans at the Battle of Magnesia, because the Syrians' huge army of elephants stampeded and smashed straight through their own ranks. Plutarch gleefully describes them as impaling soldiers on their tusks and tossing them in the air, rather like haymaking. Understandably, the Roman legions took advantage of such disarray and pressed home to victory.

Against the unsteady ranks of the Oriental armies elephant charges tended to be more effective; and before the advent of gunpowder, they carried great wooden towers on their backs, like the top deck of a bus, which could contain up to thirty archers. The elephant, however, was chiefly used by the Indian army as a battering ram, to smash down fortified defences during the final assault on a beseiged town. The gates of Indian cities were often prudently topped with huge five-foot spikes to stop the elephant bashing them down with his head.

During the wars of the Princes, elephants were used in their thousands; and there is a tragic story that after the Battle of Delhi in 1398 when the unspeakable Tamerlane trounced the Indians and captured 3,000 of their elephants, he ordered the wretched beasts to have snuff rubbed in their eyes so that they appeared to be weeping in their sorrow at being defeated.

The elephant's career as a warrior evidently ended when the generals realised his nerves were not proof against modern artillery. Three elephants in a line were prepared to pull a forty-pound siege gun to within a respectable distance of the battle, but from then onwards a team of bullocks had to take over and drag it up to the firing line.

In Rudyard Kipling's story *His Majesty Servants*, two of the gun bullocks accuse Two Tabs the elephant of being a coward. But he wisely replies: 'I can see inside my head what will happen if a shell bursts, and you bullocks can't.'

But if the elephant was no longer employed as a warrior, there was still plenty for him to do, and as we have seen it was in the Second World War in Burma that his talents were really stretched to the full. At the outbreak of war, timber became as essential a munition as steel; and elephants were employed around the clock, hauling it out of the jungle so that vast quantities could be shipped to England.

In 1942 when the Japanese swept into Burma, the elephants were hastily shifted from hauling logs to transporting as many refugees out of the country as possible. They tended not to give actual lifts to the refugees (unless they were very old or very sick), but, like imperturbable porters, were loaded up with all the food and belongings. The rest of the elephants were kept busy building bridges, making roads through the jungle, and carrying rations up to the refugee camps.

With the fall of Burma, all the elephants were seized by the Japanese. But the invading army made the fatal error of getting on the wrong side of the Burmese oozies, who at the first possible moment escaped with their elephants, usually back to the British. In December 1942, for example, a party of oozies with forty elephants had been ordered by the

Elephants carry equipment for U.S. Army troops stationed in jungle outposts through the Naga Hill region of India near the Burmese border, where American soldiers were building bases with the aid of local workers.
IWM

After the evacuation in Burma in 1941, thousands of valuable transport elephants fell into the hands of the Japanese. British officers who stayed behind, helped by local villagers, gradually rounded them up and brought them back across the Assam/Burma border to take their places alongside the allied Forces. IWM

Japanese to march to Mawlaik, but decided instead to cut and run. There were not enough oozies for all the forty animals, so their wives volunteered to bring along the riderless elephants. Acting with great courage, as they easily might have run into Japanese patrols, the party set off at night, escaping through the jungle to join Elephant Bill at Tamu. Here these forty elephants became the nucleus of No. 1 Elephant Company, Royal Indian Engineers.

Once again they were put to work, building bridges, laying log causeways through the jungle, and being the subject of endless wrangling between the sappers and the army service corps as to who had the greater claim on their services. There was no doubt that the elephant made an excellent pack animal. Unlike the mule, he didn't get bogged down in the jungle swamps, and he could carry heavier loads. Experiments were made by an anti-aircraft gun regi-

A convoy of elephants ambles down a road in central Burma, with supplies for the 36th Division advancing from Mong Mit towards Mogok. IWM ment to see if a Bofors gun could be broken down like a screw gun and carried on elephants. It was soon found that eight elephants could easily carry one gun plus a spare barrel, reserve ammunition, and all the kit for a British gun crew. Although during tests, the elephants were parked seventy-five yards from the guns and didn't flinch when they were fired, for some reason the experiments were not continued.

When his Chindits were engaged in guerrilla warfare, Wingate refused the offer of pack elephants. But in fact the only one of Wingate's columns that got all its equipment as far as the Chindwin River was the one that had secretly seconded twelve pack elephants.

Burmese oozies direct an elephant they are using to help secure timber for construction in Myitkyina, northern Burma, of an Allied supply and operations base. After the trees are cut, the elephants push the logs towards a river down which they are then floated by Myitkyina. IWM

Wingate himself obviously regretted his decision because, according to *Elephant Bill*, on the march to the Chindwin, he found a Burmese building a bridge helped by four elephants, and ordered him at revolver point to remove their harness and load them up with all his gear, including bombs and boxes of grenades. So impressed was he with these elephants, that he later insisted that the poor animals swam across the Chindwin, carrying their full loads. One wretched beast was so badly loaded that she overturned in deep water and drowned.

By 1943 more elephants escaped from the Japanese, bringing the strength of No. 1 Elephant Company up to fifty-seven. They were now building bridges along the three roads in the Kabaw Valley and also laid causeways of logs at incredible speed, rather like Sir Walter Raleigh flinging down his cloak, while whole convoys waited to pass over them.

With the arrival of the monsoon season all the army lorries got bogged down and the elephants spent their time pulling them out 'like champagne corks'. Occasionally an overhelpful driver started up his engine, and found himself towed away on a fifty-yard stampede.

During the rainy season, the elephants also provided an invaluable taxi service for the Gurkha patrols. Being an animal lover, it understandably drove 'Elephant Bill' insane with rage, when people didn't look after his precious beasts properly. Waiting for the Gurkhas to arrive, the poor elephants were often tied up for hours on end and not allowed to graze.

Even worse, the good colonel kept bumping into parties of six Gurkhas cadging a lift on one buckling, exhausted elephant, with their rifles 'slung round his ears, as though it was a hatstand'. Caught in the act, they invariably leapt off and scampered into the jungle like naughty children.

In the beginning of March 1944, the Japanese launched a major assault, but the elephants' work had become so valuable that Lt.-Col. Williams received a top secret warning to get ready in five days time to move them out of the Kabaw Valley so they didn't fall into Japanese hands. The story of how he marched the remaining forty-seven elephants over apparently im-

Horsepower gives way to elephant power – Hamburg, 1945. IWM

passable mountain tracks, climbing 5,000 feet to the same height as Hannibal, and edging along three-foot wide paths above yawning precipes, is wonderfully told in *Elephant Bill*.

The hero of the march was a handsome male 46-year-old elephant called Bandoola (named after a famous Burmese general), who was regarded by the other elephants as their commanding officer. On one particularly steep and dangerous climb, Bandoola's oozie suggested that Bandoola should lead the elephant convoy because only he knew how to close his eyes and not look down, and only he wouldn't tread on anything that wasn't safe.

Bandoola didn't let his followers down; the great beasts were pitifully slow in climbing, and Lt.-Col. Williams describes how he waited 200 yards ahead of

A jungle elephant used to haul aircraft at a Fleet Air Arm station in the Indian Ocean area, 1944. IWM the danger spot. 'After what seemed like an eternity, Bandoola's head and tusks suddenly came round the corner below me, he looked as though he was standing on his hind legs, then up came his hind quarters like a slow motion picture. The oozie was sitting on his head looking down and seeming to direct the elephant where to place each of his feet.' The back legs of many of the rest of the forty-seven who all climbed to safety, were strained to such a point that afterwards they wouldn't stop quivering.

Having reached the sanctity of Assam, Bandoola's splendidly courageous behaviour seems to have gone to his head, or rather his stomach. Shortly afterwards, he broke into a pineapple grove, and consumed 900 pineapples before he was discovered. After an understandably severe attack of colic he recovered. Sadly, in 1945, after the elephants had all been marched back to Burma, Bandoola was found murdered. Elephant Bill believed that he'd probably been shot by his oozie, who was very near retirement, and was so devoted to the elephant he couldn't bear to think of another oozie looking after him.

By this time the Japanese were beginning to lose their stranglehold on Burma, and rapidly the ranks of No. 1 Elephant Company were increased more and more by escaping elephants and their oozies. Many of the animals were very pulled down because the Japanese had overworked them appallingly and had not given them enough to eat. These had to be rested and carefully nursed back to health.

Air drops were now frequent, and a new task for the elephants was distributing the supplies. Many of the elephants, recaptured from the Japanese, were very wary of planes, having already been divebombed and machine gunned by the R.A.F. while they were carrying Japanese supplies.

After one such bombing raid, forty elephants were killed or recaptured by the British with terrible gaping wounds. As a result, the first field hospital for elephants was set up on the banks of the River Wu. Tragically, many of the wounds were caused by acid spilt from Japanese wireless batteries carried in the elephant's packs. Sometimes the acid burn was half an inch deep, and one can imagine the slow agony of the wretched animal, as the pack saddle rubbed against it. In mitigation, it must also be added that the R.A.F. loathed bombing elephant columns and many pilots asked to be excused from this very alien task. But there was no other way to stop the Japanese receiving the vital supplies carried by the elephants.

By the middle of 1945, so great had been the defections from the Japanese that the strength of No. 1 Elephant Company was up to 400. These were all kept busy twelve hours a day, building yet more bridges, often under enemy fire, and hauling the wood out of the jungle to make 541 assault boats to carry supplies across the Chindwin. Perhaps their most vital task in the whole of the war, was keeping the road from Tamu to Kalewa open during the reoccupation of Burma. This road, as an innovation, was made of waterproof hessian and 150 elephants cleared the jungle so it could be laid. By July 1945, however, having carried seven hundred tons a day for several months, some sections of the road began to crack and became flooded. The only hope of keeping it open was to build log causeways over which to divert the traffic. Five miles of these were laid by the elephants, during appalling monsoon conditions, using 12,500 huge logs. But the road was kept open, all the petrol for the army was carried over it, and Burma was retaken.

Wherever the elephant served in war he was an inspiration to men, but ironically perhaps never more to the British than when he was working for the Japanese. J.B. Bradley in his book, *Towards the Setting Sun*, describes how as a Jap prisoner-of-war he was put to work on the Burma–Thai railway felling and dragging timber.

'I suppose,' he writes, 'we were more fortunate than the men in the Southern camps in that the Japs brought in elephants to drag the timber out of the jungle. We looked on the elephants as great friends, and they provided the only material help in moving loads far beyond the capacity of sick and undernourished men.

'I think the sight of the great beasts, and the complete understanding that existed between them and their mahouts, was the only thing of beauty I can recall for the rest of my captivity.'

The Home Front

'They also Serve'

Dad's Army is one of the funniest programmes on television. But because of its deservedly universal popularity, it has given many of us the idea that life on the Home Front was a bit of a giggle. In reality, in the besieged major cities and along the South Coast, it must have been hell on earth with appalling disasters like the 1982 Hyde Park car bomb where animals were horribly mutilated becoming an everyday occurrence.

For a dog or a cat too, London in the blitz must have been a hundred times worse than being let loose on

Guy Fawkes night. Even if one bears in mind that a dog or cat's hearing and sensitivity to vibration are far more acute than our own, it is difficult for a human to appreciate what animals were subjected to. Suddenly to fear and often hunger were added the inexplicable roaring from the skies, the earsplitting explosions, the collapsing blazing masonry, while a direct hit on the house in which they lived would rob them of all the family they knew and loved.

We can therefore be thankful that vigorous animal welfare societies – the R.S.P.C.A. and P.D.S.A., the Canine Defence League and the National A.R.P. for Animals Committee – were all at the ready to cope with such disasters, and between 1939 and 1945 rescued an incredible 256,000 animals and birds from bombing raids.

I shall concentrate in this chapter on World War II, because it was the first war in which this country was subjected to large-scale bombing. As usual in the years before war broke out, the War Office put their heads in

'Give me the R.S.P.C.A.' – a bombed-out parrot with ruffled feathers. BRISTOL EVENING POST

This P.D.S.A. centre was destroyed by bombing during the London blitz; but work carried on from a mobile unit.

Helpers and inmates line up outside the P.D.S.A. receiving station. IWM

the sand, and it was left to the R.S.P.C.A. to try and shake them out of their apathy. How, demanded the R.S.P.C.A., were they intending in the face of major bombing raids to protect the 40,000 horses, 9,000 cattle, 6,000 sheep, 18,000 pigs, 400,000 dogs (only including those who had licenses) and approximately 1,500,000 cats who lived in Greater London alone. The War Office shrugged their shoulders helplessly at such a monumental problem, rather in the same way that we today would react if asked how we would cope with all the animal casualties in the event of a nuclear attack. Not getting any cooperation, the R.S.P.C.A. retired, and produced a leaflet in 1937, telling people how to look after their animals in air raids. It became an immediate bestseller, and went into six editions.

Fortunately also, between the wars, the R.S.P.C.A. and the P.D.S.A. (founded by Mrs Dickin of medal fame) had built up a network of more than a hundred clinics to look after sick and homeless animals. It was easy for these to turn themselves into clinics for the wounded, but tragically their first task was largely unnecessary. In the first four days after war broke out, such was the mass hysteria that 400,000 cats and dogs in the London area alone were brought in to be put down. This caused inseparable problems. Not only had the clinics to hold the hands of the heartbroken owners, but also to dispose of all the bodies – no easy task when their foundries had to be dowsed at sunset because of the blackout.

Then there was the headache of London's huge horse population – what was to happen to the 4,000 cobs, for example, who pulled milk floats every day. The

Form pinned to the gatepost, showing the number of people and animals sleeping in a house, which was issued by the National Canine Defence League and the R.S.P.C.A. IWM

IMPORTANT!

NO. OF PERSONS SLEEPING IN THIS HOUSE

DOG / CAT
(Cross out whichever is inapplicable)

ALSO IN

HOUSE

HIS BED IS

(State location of bed as exactly as possible.)

Issued by

The National Canine Defence League, Victoria Station House, S.W.1.	The Royal Society for the Prevention of Cruelty to Animals, 105, Jermyn Street, S.W.1.

public were asked to lend their garages, often empty because cars had been requisitioned, as a temporary refuge for any horse caught on the road during an air raid. King George VI set an excellent example by offering the Royal Mews for this purpose. And many a humble milkhorse, rescued from a blazing stable, found a luxurious temporary home, in stables that had once housed the illustrious Windsor Greys.

People were issued with shelter cards to pin on their gateposts, to show they would give sanctuary to dogs and their owners caught out walking during a raid. Pet-owners were issued with another card to put outside their house, stating how many people slept there, how many animals, and in which room they usually slept, so the rescue squads might have some hint of where to seek out casualties if the house were hit.

But these were merely precautions. Soon the bombs rained down and the real work began as, night and morning, rescue squads raced their animal ambulances over roads scattered with broken glass and rubble, digging out terrified animals trapped under buildings, giving first aid to the injured and gathering up the homeless. After a raid, every bomb site would be haunted by cats and dogs searching hopelessly for their lost homes and owners, and waiting in dread for the next night's raid.

Time and again, the rescue squads risked their lives. One street was evacuated because a score of unexploded time bombs had fallen. An R.S.P.C.A. inspector calmly went in, searching each house and coming away with four cats, three dogs and a cage of budgerigars. On another occasion, the last animal to be rescued was a budgerigar; as he was carried out of the devastated tenement in his cage, he was heard to remark in ringing tones, 'This is my night out.'

One of the greatest services the inspectors did was to provide comfort for animal owners hurt in air raids. Lying in hospital, fretting about the fate of their pets, many a victim was made happier by being able to pencil a shaky note to the local R.S.P.C.A. man asking him to keep a lookout. Imagine their relief at knowing that Blackie the cat had been found and was being temporarily housed in a kind foster home, or even that Spot, the blind old terrier, had been so badly injured that he'd been put out of his misery.

No creature was too small or unimportant for the R.S.P.C.A. One moment they were reassuring some old lady that her bees really didn't need a gas mask, the next, receiving a letter of thanks for retrieving a little water tortoise from a bombed-out garden. There was even a woman inspector who drove through the East End every day, collecting cats from smouldering office buildings and warehouses. So great was the East Enders' faith in her that if they got bombed out of their houses, they left their dogs tied to the gatepost, knowing she would take care of them all.

A joyful reunion.

One of the worst jobs for the rescue squads was working in clinics along the South Coast, where ambulance drivers raced at their peril through blacked-out streets with the anti-aircraft guns pounding overhead. They were continually on call to lonely farms. In Kent alone, 100 horses, 500 cattle, and thousands of sheep were killed by doodlebugs and rockets. The greatest problem was digging out desperately wounded animals at night in the pitch blackout, when only an occasional torch beam or a lighted match was allowed.

But however hard the rescue squads worked, they only relied on sight and common sense. The dog, on the other hand, is guided by his nose and that wonderful sixth sense that is so often given to animals. Beauty was the wirehaired terrier mascot of the P.D.S.A. Rescue Squad. One day she accompanied her master and his mates, who were hoping to dig out some missing people, to a bomb site. Beauty got bored and wandered off. Then rather like the boy at Rugby School who suddenly seized the ball and ran, thus inventing Rugby football, the little dog started digging. So vigorous were her scrabblings, and the showers of stones that were being sent in all directions, that her master and the squad came to her aid. After some strenuous excavation, a cat was discovered unhurt but terrified under a splintered table. From then on Beauty was constantly in work. She found no fewer than 63 casualties, and won herself a Dickin Medal. She always scrabbled so energetically that her little paws became raw and bleeding, so her admirers bought her some leather boots.

Another amateur rescue dog, whose heroic work also won him a Dickin Medal was a little mongrel called Rip, the mascot of the A.R.P. at Poplar. Having been found homeless and starving after a heavy raid in

Victims of the Blitz: Beauty, the P.D.S.A. mascot,
with some of the dogs she rescued.

Rip, the little mongrel mascot of the A.R.P. at Poplar, was himself found homeless and starving, and spent the rest of his wartime career rescuing other casualties.

1940, Rip obviously thought it was his duty to rescue others and was soon sniffing out casualties trapped under buildings. How welcome to the victims must have been the first sounds of those scrabbling paws and shrill terrier yaps, and the first sight of the grinning Tommy Brock face with its merry friendly eyes.

Such were Rip and Beauty's fame that towards the end of the war, the authorities decided to train dogs officially to trace casualties. Out of fourteen dogs who were posted to work in London, five of them – Jet, Irma, Peter, Thorn and Rex – all won Dickin Medals. The dog's worst fear in life is fire, which is why Londoners owe such a debt to their rescue dogs, who battled through blazing, collapsing buildings, choked by smoke, and often repeatedly sick from gas leaks.

Jet, a noble and beautiful black Alsatian, for example, arrived having been violently car sick on the 100-mile drive to London. He was immediately put to work on a house in the suburbs which had suffered a direct hit, and found the person who was missing. On another occasion, he discovered twenty-five people trapped under the same rubble.

Irma, another beautiful Alsatian, also saved numerous lives. Once she seemed certain that someone was trapped under a collapsed building and refused to leave the spot. Extremely sceptical, the rescue squad fol-

Five courageous dogs whose rescue work locating trapped victims of bombings during World War II won them all Dickin Medals. Top, l. to r.: *Rex and Thorn;* bottom, l. to r.: *Irma, Beauty, and Jet.* All IWM lowed her lead, and eventually dug out two little girls, both alive. Irma's great gift was to know if the casualty she'd located were alive or not. If the former, she would bark joyously, but if they were dead, after giving one quick wag to acknowledge their presence underground, when they were finally dug out, she would frantically lick the lifeless face or hand, gazing up at her handler, entreating him to make them better.

It is nice to know that these splendidly dedicated animals had the odd lapse. Taylor and Peter, two of the most consistent dogs, were once taken to the site of a fallen rocket. On arrival they staged a sit-down strike. Neither would budge. Worried they were ill, their handlers took them home. It was only on reflection that Taylor's handler remembered that although the dogs were usually fed horsemeat and biscuits, during the last few days, the meat hadn't arrived, so they were making do with biscuits and water. Once the meat ration was restored, both dogs voted to go back to work.

It was remarkable how continuously animals' sixth sense was put to good use throughout the war years. One farmer in the Northeast, on the day war broke out, said that early the same morning he couldn't understand why all the animals were so quiet. There was no mooing, no crowing, no farm dogs barking – nothing. He and his family were quite sure the animals sensed something terrible was about to happen.

There are also endless wonderful stories of the way in which dogs warned their owners that a raid was imminent, waking them up, pulling off the bedclothes, and rounding them into the shelter, only a few minutes before the siren went. As an added bonus, the families were usually able to go to bed before the all clear went. The dog would suddenly get up, leave the shelter, and settle into its basket with a contented sigh. Five minutes later the all clear would sound. One little dog called Dee often stayed curled up in her basket when the siren went, and invariably no planes came over. Equally, when there was no warning siren she often became very agitated, and urged everyone to take cover, and sure enough a sneak raider would arrive, or an unexpected raid on a much larger scale would take place.

In times of war too, animals normally antagonistic seem to sign a secret truce. When one large bomb fell in the Hendon area, an inspector commandeered a car, filled it with cats, dogs, pet rabbits and budgerigars, and housed them in his own drawing-room until proper arrangements could be made. No Tweetie Pie–Sylvester scuffles took place between any of the animals.

It was touching too how animals helped each other. Towards the end of the war, one family cat had kittens. Whenever there was a raid, Jackie, the resident brown and white mongrel, always carried these kittens down one by one to the shelter, with the cat walking alongside, mewing and supervising. After the all clear, however, Jackie retired to bed, and left the cat to carry home her own kittens.

Cats seemed to be more upset at being bombed out of their homes than dogs, because they are deeply attached to certain territory, whereas the dog tends to attach himself to certain people, and be happy wherever they are. One remarkable example of sixth sense and heroism was shown by Faith, the beautiful tabby cat who belonged to the vicar of St Augustine's Church, Watling Street. Normally Faith slept upstairs in the vicarage but on 6 September 1940 she became restless and suddenly lifted her kitten out of its basket and carried it three floors downstairs, where she put it in a pigeonhole in the wall where music was stored. Four times the vicar tried to take the kitten upstairs and each time Faith brought it back so the vicar gave orders that the pigeonhole should be cleared and the cat's basket put there. Faith immediately settled in happily. Three days later when the vicar was away from home, the vicarage was bombed. The moving inscription under Faith's picture in the church tells the rest of the story:

Our dear little church cat, the bravest cat in all the world. On Monday September 9, 1940, she endured perils and horrors beyond the power of words to tell. Shielding her kitten in a sort of recess (a spot she selected three days before the tragedy occurred) she sat through the whole frightful night of bombing and fire, guarding her little kitten.

The roofs and masonry exploded. The whole house blazed.

Faith, who protected her little kiiten through a fearful night of bombing and fire, clearly demonstrates her beauty and sweet nature here.

Floors fell through in front of her. Fire and water and ruin were all around her. Yet she stayed calm and steadfast, and waited for help. We rescued her in the early morning, while the place was still burning, and by the mercy of the Almighty God, she and her kitten were not only saved, but unhurt. God be praised and thanked for his goodness and mercy to our little pet.

Horses, as was shown earlier often have psychic gifts. One police horse, Ubique, was trotting through London towards the end of the war, when suddenly, as he was entering a main road from a side road, he dug his heels in and refused to go on. Puzzled, his rider didn't force him. A few seconds later, a flying bomb landed in the middle of the main road, in the direction they were going, on precisely the spot they would have reached.

At the beginning of the war, to avoid the danger, all the police horses and several stable cats were evacuated out of London to Kempton Park and other stables. For several months, their policeman riders ate their hearts out, longing to be back on duty, and finally were allowed to return, with all the horses and a vastly increased population of stable cats.

As Dorothea St Hill Bourne points out in her

enchanting history of the P.D.S.A. *They Also Serve*, police horses are trained to cope with crowd noises and revolver fire. But nothing could have prepared them for the thunder of the gun batteries (in Hyde Park alone, there were 132 rocket guns, near the police stables) together with the shriek and crash of bombs, the roar of land mines and rockets, and the terrifying rattle of flying bombs.

In order that these raids should be connected in the horses' minds with something pleasant, they were given an extra feed whenever the siren went. This cured any sign of panic, but had a disastrous effect on the horses' waistline, so the feeds were discontinued. The horses were outraged – what was the point of hearing a gong without getting one's dinner – and made the most frightful uproar everytime the siren went and no snack was forthcoming.

Three horses, Olga, Upstart and Regal all won Dickin Medals. The first two were awarded for unquestionable steadfastness on duty. When bombs fell nearby showering them with broken glass and metal, both horses carried on calmly setting an example to everyone, as their riders directed the traffic. Regal kept his nerve twice when his stable was bombed. The first time, he stayed calm as the flames drew nearer and nearer; the second, the roof caved in on top of him. Nor should these police horses be written off as phlegmatic and insensitive. Those who worked with them throughout the war said that, although they remained rocklike in a crisis, they became very edgy in the stables and would start as some car backfired or a door slammed, sounds they would have ignored in peacetime.

As food rationing began to bite in World War II, feeding animals became more and more of a problem. Working horses had an official protein ration as did cattle, chickens and goats. Hay was never rationed, but was often of poor quality and in very short supply. Many of the larger horses and those unfortunate riding school hacks who didn't qualify for extra rations must have gone dreadfully short.

If it hadn't been for the truly backbreaking efforts of the Women's Land Army, things might have become very serious. These heroic girls often started work at five in the morning, and during double summer time didn't knock off until eleven at night. Not only did they make hay, plough the fields, harvest the corn, hoe endless fields of kale and turnips, and feed pigs with swill that floated with dead rats, but they also had to milk the cows. The stories of exhausted landgirls were almost as universal as the pigeon jokes. My favourite was of a kindly cow, who as the weary landgirl staggered in to milk her, said sympathetically: 'You just hang on, dearie, and I'll jump up and down.'

Many people kept hens to boost the family egg ration. Consequently grain became short, and the Government was forced to restrict supplies. Once again the R.S.P.C.A. stepped in, suggesting that people should feed their chickens on weed seeds, berries and nuts, and drew up a leaflet telling people which seeds and berries were poisonous and which not. By an odd coincidence, it was discovered that a government committee was drawing up a paper on the same subject, but displaying an uncharacteristic sense of humour, they suggested the war would be over before their paper was ready and urged the R.S.P.C.A. to go ahead with theirs.

Realising what a boost people get from their canaries and budgies, and how even thrushes and robins visiting a bird table after a night of horror could raise the spirits, the R.S.P.C.A. also produced two further leaflets telling people how to grow bird seed and how to find the sort of weeds suitable for the bird table.

In the First World War, as early as 1915, the anti-dog lobby went on the rampage. Reports started appearing in the press castigating the dog for being a national danger because he ate food that could have saved human lives. Later in the war, when enemy submarines had sunk several merchant ships, causing further food shortages, the anti-dog lobby really got into its stride, and managed to persuade the Government to draw up a scheme to destroy half the dogs in England, which included stepping up the licence fee and drastically reducing breeding. Fortunately the National Canine Defence League carried on such a

Olga, Upstart, and Regal, three brave police horses who won the Dickin Medal.

There was plenty of work for horses on the land on the Home Front – but not much food, judging by the prominent ribs. IWM

formidable campaign against this scheme – pointing out that the dog was a protection and a comfort to lonely war widows, that men at the front were longing to see their pets when they came home, and that anyway the dogs usually survived on scraps – that eventually the Government scrapped the idea and even agreed to issue more food suitable for dogs.

Early in World War I, the Canine Defence League also discovered that families of men serving in the Army and Navy were being advised to put down their dogs because they couldn't afford to feed or license them. The League promptly advertised in the press and on posters, and wrote to the commanding officers of many regiments, saying they would be willing to help such families keep their dogs. An appeal was launched for funds, and soon the tenderhearted British people were responding, often through their pets. Thus in the Canine Defence accounts, you find records of 'an elderly doggie' contributing one shilling, and the 'family cat' coughing up 1s. 6d. Max 'an old pug dog' gave 7s. 6d, while 'two well cared for dogs' really pushed out the boat and sent £1 each. Soon soldiers' families all over the country were receiving regular supplies of dog biscuits, and by the end of the war the League had paid for 11,707 licences for soldiers' dogs. In the Second World War, the anti-dog brigade started agitating again. This time the R.S.P.C.A. came to the rescue with yet another leaflet advising the public how to feed their dogs without depriving humans. Recipe suggestions included gravy and dog biscuits, boiled rice and gravy, brown bread baked in the oven, tinned dog food, horsemeat, and sheep's windpipe and stomach. The fact that people were prepared to queue for long hours to buy horsemeat at 8d a pound for their pets proved their devotion.

Cats were also hit by rationing. They must survive, said the Government, on water; and it became illegal to give a cat milk although, after some heavy lobbying, warehouse mousers and sick cats were allowed their ration of dried milk.

One small feline, known as Cat, belonged to a war widow, who had to support her 10-year-old son. One day Cat was informed by her sorrowing mistress that she would have to be put down tomorrow as the family couldn't afford to feed her anymore. Little Cat obviously digested this information, if nothing else, that night, and next day she went out and returned with a dead wild rabbit, intact except for a small bite in the throat. For the rest of the war, Cat supplemented the family larder at least three times a week, often bringing in rabbits much bigger than herself, and always waiting patiently for her share.

Mascots

'The friendship of a dog is precious. It becomes even more so when one is so far removed from home as we are in Africa. I have a Scottie. In him I find consolation and diversion . . . he is the "one person" to whom, I can talk without the conversation coming back to the war.'

General Eisenhower writing home during World War II.

One of my favourite Imperial War Museum photographs was taken towards the end of World War I, and shows a group of exhausted soldiers snatching a moment's respite in the ruins of a bombed house. One of them, like a child cuddling a teddy bear, holds a little white mongrel in his arms, while the dog's head rests on his shoulder with a look of infinite trust on its face. For men so far from home – lonely, frightened, under constant threat of death, and deprived of family or girlfriends – a pet who could unstintingly receive and return affection, must have provided immeasurable comfort. Thus among the unsung heroes of the war are all those mascots who rallied everyone's spirits and brought a note of comedy to the grim opera of war.

The mascot's function was also to bring luck. As a child clutches a tiny black china cat before going into an exam, so the regimental pet became a symbol of good fortune that would bring the regiment or company safely out of the war. One remembers Boy, another little white dog, who accompanied Prince Rupert into battle, and who always seemed to bring good luck to the Cavaliers. The Roundheads, on the other hand regarded the dog as an evil spirit, and cheered when he was killed in 1644 at the battle of Marston Moor. From that moment, the Cavaliers' fortunes plummeted.

The Roundheads used to scoff at Prince Rupert's devotion to his dog, and how he always slept with Boy in his arms at night. But just as a mascot cheers up the soldiers, a favourite animal can assuage the loneliness of the man in high command. Eisenhower, for example, was devoted to his Scottie, who accompanied him on campaigns and was, Ike admitted, the only living thing he could talk to in the evenings who didn't want to discuss the war. Even Hitler was besotted with his Alsatian, Blondi, and spent hours romping with him, and teaching him new tricks.

Allenby found relief from the pressure of the desert campaign through his great interest in birds. He even stationed a Yorkshire sergeant permanently at a watering place frequented by migrating birds; and whenever a new species turned up, the Commander-in-Chief would forget the cares of the campaign, and slip off to see the bird for himself.

A soldier in the ruins of the French town of Athies finds comfort in holding a little dog (1917). IWM

In the same way Lowell Thomas, in his nature notes on the First World War, quoted an officer who wrote home about the 'nightingales singing most rippingly at the front' and how a devastated wood harboured pheasant, green woodpeckers, tree creepers and the usual thrushes and black birds.

'It is a strange place for them to choose', the officer went on, 'but it is very comforting to hear some of the old familiar woodland sounds again.'

It was this desire for familiarity and comfort, plus the fact that no British soldier can bear to see an animal or bird lost or ill-treated, that lead him to turn local strays into company mascots wherever he went.

In *They Also Serve*, Dorothea St Hill Bourne draws a touching picture of a scene during the retreat from the Quattara Depression and El Alamein, 'when the streets of Cairo were filled with lorry loads of troops, bearded and dusty from days of hard fighting, with their pets sitting beside them, or riding on the roof of the lorry.'

It is hard for us today to appreciate how war must have terrified the wild animals. A friend told me that when her father joined his regiment at Mersa Matruh, during the fighting in the Western Desert, the bombardment had been raging for days. The second night he was there, he just crashed out on the sand from sheer exhaustion, while the battle roared on all around him. Waking in the morning, he felt something warm pressing against the back of his legs and, opening his eyes, he saw a desert fox creeping away from where it had spent the night, sheltering in terror from the noise. Desert foxes are desperately shy animals, who normally won't come near humans, which made the whole episode all the more pathetic.

Happily several desert foxes, generally cubs who had lost their mothers, were tamed and made excellent mascots. Other rescued wild animals who followed the drum included wild boars, mongeese, antelopes, prairie wolves, a kagu, several panthers, bears and tigers, a baby porcupine, a hyena, a jackal, a nylghau and a llama, to mention only a few.

Mascots, in fact, ranged from the sublime to the very ridiculous. Throughout the First World War one soldier kept a scorpion in a pickle jar, while in the Second World War, a G.I. brought over a goldfish in a whiskey bottle, which spent the entire Northwest European campaign swimming around in a tin helmet.

How some of the mascots were acquired is interesting. One black hen was swapped for an old pair of trousers, and in gratitude provided the company with eggs for the rest of the war, while Charlotte, the famous mascot of *H.M.S. Cadmus*, joined the ship at Biarritz in exchange for four tins of sardines for a native boatman. Charlotte, who started off as Charlie, and only revealed her sex by laying a huge egg, went through the invasion of Sicily and Salerno, and was always the first to hear enemy aircraft and give the alarm. Like many mascots, she also knew the difference between friend and foe. If an Italian got within three or four feet of the ship, she'd open her wings and threaten to fly at him.

One of the first and most famous mascots was Jacob, the goose of the Coldstream Guards. In 1837, when the British were trying to keep down the Canadian rebels in Quebec, Guardsman John Kemp was on sentry duty, and saw a large goose waddling past, which suddenly froze in its tracks. Following its small-eyed gaze, Kemp saw a large fox stealthily approaching. Next moment the goose had sought refuge between Kemp's legs, and realising if he fired a shot it would wake the whole battalion, Kemp coolly bayonetted the fox. The grateful goose rubbed his head against Kemp's knee like a friendly cat, and from then on protected the garrison better than any guard dog. On one occasion, when sound of the approaching rebels was muffled by the snow, Jacob frantically squawked the alarm, and woke the guard in time. For this brave act he was presented with a golden collar; and when the regiment eventually returned to England Jacob came too, and became a great friend of the Duke of Wellington. His head, wearing the golden collar, can still be seen in the regimental headquarters of the Coldstream Guards in Birdcage Walk.

The Boer War produced two dog mascots of great character. Scout was a little terrier bitch picked up by the 1st Royal Dragoons, who always marched twenty yards in front of the regiment, barking at everything from bullocks to the Boer's famous big gun at Spion

Bamse was the St. Bernard mascot of fighting ship Thorod *in the Royal Norwegian Navy. After the German invasion of his country, Bamse escaped with his master.*

Kop. One day she disappeared, and such was the regard in which she was held by her regiment, that the colonel, Lord Basing, sent a search party to look for her. A few miles back, they discovered Scout rushing about in great excitement, having given birth to two puppies which she'd housed in a hole. She was only too happy for the troopers to pick them up, but scorned a lift herself, barking joyfully as the little cavalcade caught up with the rest of the soldiers.

Scout's story is told in more detail in an enchanting book called *Mascots and Pets of the Services* by Major T.J. Edwards. For her services during the war, she was awarded the Queen's Medal with six bars, and the King's Medal with two bars. Rather more reprehensibly, she slept with a different soldier every night.

According to Major Edwards, she finally died while with the regiment in India in 1904. Two days after she was buried she was disinterred and stuffed, but the native taxidermist 'made such a hideous job of it, lengthening her body, giving her stick-like legs, a snarling expression and ferocious eyes, that the idea was abandoned.... For many years Scout was mourned by her regiment. For pluck and endurance, faithfulness and affection a better example it would be hard to find.'

Billy, a brindle bull terrier who was attached to the Royal Ulster Rifles for fifteen years, also went through the Boer War. The company often used to ride fifty miles in a day, and Billy would limp along on three legs holding up his paw in the most pathetic manner, until one of the men took pity on him and hoisted him up into the saddle. When the regiment returned to Dover, Billy disgraced himself by attacking a citizen – no doubt thinking him an awful Boer – and was banished to a farm. There he pined for his soldier friends and refused to eat so he was eventually allowed back again.

In the Second World War Bamse, the vast St Bernard mascot of the Norwegian fighting ship *Thorod*, was also confined to ship, but this time for fighting another dog. The minute he managed to jump ship, however, Bamse tracked down his former enemy and, picking him up by the scruff of the neck, calmly dropped him into the harbour.

Bamse redeemed himself by his great sense of responsibility. When his shipmates were ashore, he always worried that they might not get back in time, and toured the local dives rounding them up. He knew all their favourite cafes, and would often board the right bus to take him to more distant haunts.

Cats, as was pointed out in the chapter on the Home Front, tend to become even more attached to territory than to people, which is why they are a better mascot for a ship, than for a regiment which is always travelling overland. Often they refused to leave their ships at all. One cat called Susan, who served on a Royal Navy tank landing craft, was absolutely terrified when she was demobbed and had her first experience of dry land. Grass in particular scared the life out of her, and she took a long time to settle down to a land lubber existence.

Cats also performed a valuable service on board ship keeping the rats down. Evidently a really good ratter who started off as ordinary ship's cat could rise from the ranks, and be promoted to mascot of a particular part of the ship, perhaps the engine room, and even finally reach the dizzy heights of being mascot of the whole ship. Whiskey, a splendid tabby and mascot of

Three feline mascots. Above left*: Whiskey, ship's tabby of the* HMS Duke of York *– remembered both for her ratting prowess and for having slept soundly through the battle in which the German cruiser* Scharnhorst *was sunk;* right*: Susan, who served in a landing craft and was present for the assault on Normandy,* IWM Facing page*: the kitten mascot of* HMS Belfast (HMS Belfast)

H.M.S. Duke of York, however, only distinguished herself by sleeping soundly through the action in which her ship sank the German battlecruiser *Scharnhorst*. It was the hour for her afternoon sleep, and even the roar of the guns didn't wake her.

Sadly, pets often outgrew their welcome on board battleships and cruisers, and were shunted off by harassed captains to the Navy Zoo at Whale Island, Portsmouth. A bear cub makes an amusing pet aboard a seagoing ship – until it is strong enough to escape or eat the crew. Bruno, bear mascot on board *H.M.S. Aboukir*, slipped his chain when the Russian ship *Nicholas II* was in dry dock, and proceeded to climb the aft bridge, scramble along the awning, tear down the ensign, and terrorise the crew in the process.

Poilu, the lion mascot of 19th British division in World War I, became so tame that he followed General Bridges around like a dog. This somewhat unnerved visitors. Asquith, being taken up to the top of Scherrenberg Hill to see the famous view of the front line, suddenly clapped his hands over his eyes, crying, 'I may be imagining things, but did I just see a lion in the path?' Poor Poilu was shortly afterwards court martialled and sent to Maidstone Zoo.

One of the most enchanting mascots was Voytek, the Syrian bear, whose funny, moving story is told in *Soldier Bear* by Weislaw Lasocki and Geoffrey Morgan. Voytek was remarkable in that even when he grew up he never became savage or reverted to his wild animal nature. He was discovered as a baby by the Second Polish Transport Company, when they were driving through northern Persia towards Palestine. Having lost his mother, he immediately attached himself to Lance Corporal Peter Prendys, who fed him on condensed milk and gave him an old washing up bowl to sleep in. Voytek soon took on many human characteristics, including crying like a baby whenever his master left him.

His most famous misdeed was when the company moved to Quisal Rabat in Iraq in 1942, where a section of the Women's Signal Corps were also camped. One afternoon Voytek took a stroll round the base and, coming across a lot of flimsy female underclothes on a line, proceeded to tug them off and

Andrew, a fawn and white wartime stray, was accepted as mascot of the Mascot Club.

wrap them round his head. Then uprooting the clothes prop, he marched up and down trailing the rest of the shredded underwear as though he were trooping the colour. When his master bawled him out later, poor Voytek sat with his great front paws over his eyes, until the girls of Signal Corps forgave him, and gave him sweets to cheer him up. At Christmas he was given cakes, figs and dates, all beautifully wrapped up, but bored with the thought of unpacking them, he ate the paper as well. Later in the day, he was given a slug of white wine, and liked it so much he drained the whole bottle, followed by a bottle of beer. After everyone had gone to bed, a drunken Voytek broke into the storeroom, and stuffed himself with jam, fruit juice and honey before passing out.

One of his favourite pastimes, apart from travelling in the truck beside his master, was swimming in the sea, where he would invariably surface in the centre of a shrieking crowd of female bathers. When it grew very hot in the summer, he learnt to work the shower, and used it so often that the Nissen hut had to be locked to prevent him exhausting the Company's entire water supply. On one occasion, Voytek was delighted to find the door ajar. Bustling into the hut, he discovered a cowering Arab who'd come to spy out the lie of the land for a raiding party, intending to steal all the company's weapons and ammunition. As a result, the Arab spy confessed all and the raiding party were rounded up. Voytek became a hero and was given two bottles of beer, and allowed to spend all morning splashing happily in the bath hut.

When the company reached Italy, he saw serious action for the first time, but soon got used to planes roaring overhead and bombs exploding. One day when his truck was being unloaded, he got out of the passenger seat, walked up to one of the soldiers, and solemnly held out his paws. From then on he helped to unload boxes of ammunition and huge cannon shells.

At the end of the war, Voytek marched like a soldier through the cheering streets of Glasgow, and enjoyed a posting in Scotland, where he helped break up firewood, carry logs to the cookhouse, move crates and roll barrels. Sadly in 1947 his master was demobbed, and had absolutely no way of keeping Voytek. Heartbroken, he was forced to hand him over to Edinburgh Zoo. Voytek evidently walked into his life imprisonment cage like a lamb. But the zoo director wrote afterwards, 'I never felt so sorry to see an animal who had enjoyed so much fun and freedom, confined to a cage.'

It is now time perhaps in this chapter to praise once again the R.S.P.C.A. and the P.D.S.A., as well as the zoos, who so often gave sanctuary to these animal mascots, when they fell ill, or when their masters moved on and could no longer look after them. In *They Also Serve*, Dorothea St Hill Bourne describes how the animals brought into the P.D.S.A. hospital in Cairo had often been adopted by a whole unit, and the patient would be accompanied by a deputation of men:

> A truck once arrived at the hospital, and out got eight large soldiers, and a corporal carrying a small rough brown and white mongrel and her five puppies. The bitch had served at Benghazi, Greece, Crete, Syria and Palestine, now the patrol had been posted to an unknown destination where no dogs were allowed. Would the P.D.S.A. put her to sleep, or dispose of the family, if the platoon didn't return? Alas none of them did, but the little dog eventually found a home with another soldier.

In the same way, the R.S.P.C.A. realised how much these mascots meant to the men, and paid the quarantine fee of many a pet that was brought home. Similarly, when a regiment stationed in England was sent abroad, someone had to take care of all the stray animals, who'd been encouraged to make the camp their own.

The army moved on, but it was the animal welfare societies, the zoos, and to a certain extent the R.A.V.C., who were left to pick up the pieces. They did this because they realised – as did many commanding officers – how a mascot boosted the soldiers' morale.

Minnie, for example, the pony mascot of the 1st Battalion of the Lancashire Fusiliers, was born in Burma in 1944, during a heavy Japanese raid. As the bombs crashed all around, she was delivered by Sergeant Lee. The troops were enchanted to hear of her safe arrival – it was such a relief from all the death and

Dogs, accompanied by their owners, queue up to join the P.D.S.A. Mascot Club.

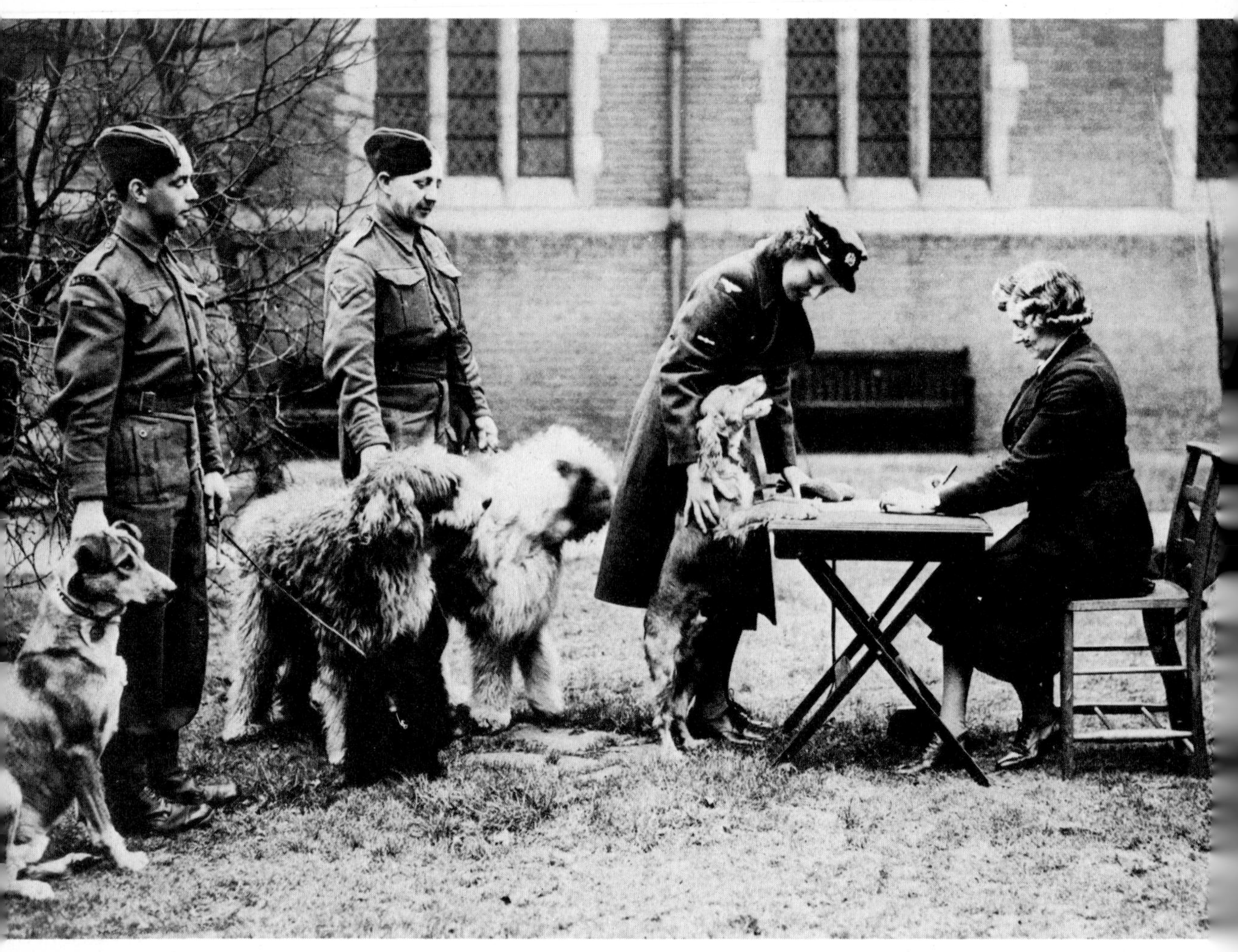

destruction – and soon royal bulletins were being issued as to Minnie's health.

Later during another heavy bombardment, a mule kicked little Minnie in the eye. Again Sergeant Lee worked long and heroically and managed to save the eye. Brigadier 'Mad Mike' Calvert (last seen praising an exhausted soldier in the chapter on the mule) ordered reports of her condition to be sent to all forward positions. As Minnie recovered, so did the morale of the troops.

Eventually she came to run the battalion single-hoofed, entering the sergeants' mess on many occasions, and devouring everything in sight, including a tablecloth. Once, during the adjutant's drill parade, she decided to join Sergent Lee on parade, and kept prodding him in the back. So convulsed was everyone with mirth, that eventually the adjutant dismissed the parade. Minnie's reputation rocketed; who else could get the battalion off drill parade 35 minutes early?

Such was her popularity that when it was time for the battalion to return to England in 1947, a 'Minnie' fund was set up to pay for her fare. She enjoyed the trip

Field-Marshal Montgomery and Lt.-Col. R.C. MacDonald, commanding the 2nd Battalion Royal Warwicks, with regimental mascot 'Bobbie'.

enormously, virtually dining at the Captain's table every night and sampling everything from spam to condensed milk. Later back home, she took her place at the head of the battalion, wearing a handsome saddlecloth and gaiters in old rose and primrose.

Many mascots cheered up the troops by their continual defiance of authority. One regiment had a fox called Freddie, who was utterly charming to Churchill, but took a large bite out of Monty. There was also Bobbie, a very overindulged antelope belonging to the 2nd Battalion of the Royal Warwickshire Regiment, who according to *Mascots and Pets of the Services* disgraced himself on parade during a tattoo performance. 'Used to leading the battalion, he was furious at being behind a large well covered drum major, instead of ahead of the massed bands and drums. With great cunning he bided his time, then butted this gorgeous individual from behind, tearing his trousers. After this Bobbie was allowed to lead.' Goats, not unlike mules, are such idiosyncratic creatures that you have to know them personally to appreciate their finer qualities. One of the most bizarre

Goats, despite their refractory behaviour, have many fans – as can be seen from this solemn funeral of ex-Flight Sergeant Lewis, the mascot of the RAF Association.

photographs in the Imperial War Museum shows us the funeral of ex-Flight Sergeant Lewis, the goat mascot of the R.A.F. Association, at Ilford. A group of men from the P.D.S.A. in white coats, are gravely carrying the coffin, followed by terribly sad looking R.A.F. top brass carrying wreaths, with a large and tearful crowd bringing up the rear.

Nor is it just the English who love their goats. *Animal World*, the R.S.P.C.A. magazine, tells the story of an Indian soldier in the First World War who one day, in the thick of the battle, saw that the company goat had strayed into the firing line. Realising its terror, the Sikh rushed out above the trenches into a hail of bullets to rescue it. He managed to reach the goat, and was just leading it to safety when a shell killed them both.

Equally, when the 5th Canadian Infantry Battalion were sent to the front, they were told that Sergeant Billy, their goat mascot must be left behind in Canada. This caused an uproar, 'We can get another colonel,' said the soldiers unanimously, 'but not another goat!' Billy was subsequently smuggled on board ship wrapped in a tarpaulin and hidden in a wagon. Arriving in France, he proved even more insubordinate than Bobbie the antelope. On one occasion he was discovered by the battalion Sergeant-Major chewing up the Nominal roll. In attempting to rescue it, this august individual found himself butted out of the tent. During the second battle of Ypres, Billy was wounded by shrapnel and, so his rescuers report, was found standing guard over a terrified Prussian officer.

Charlie, the goat mascot of the 2nd Battalion of the Welsh Regiment also had a voracious appetite. In India in 1943, he ate the adjutant's pyjamas, and then more seriously moved onto a gunner subaltern's identity card and and ten rupee notes for pudding. Loss of an identity card is a court martial offence, but evidence of Charlie's habits were enough to exonerate the gunner subaltern. Alas, the adjutant was still smarting over the loss of his pyjamas, and condemned poor Charlie to the stewpot.

The 95th Foot Regiment always had ram mascots called Derby. Derby VIII turned out to be an atheist who refused to attend church parades and frequently charged the band when they were playing religious music. In the end, God struck Derby VIII down and he died in 1893 of ingrowing horns.

By contrast the Royal Inniskillings had a pig mascot called Muriel who was very religious. According to the *Spring of Shillelah*, the Inniskilling journal, Muriel had to be tied up on Sunday to prevent her joining both Church of England and Roman Catholic parades. Sometimes she broke loose and made for the church, and during a dull sermon, the men would be thrown into fits of laughter hearing Muriel's grunting approach. Next moment she would be inside, showing her delight at being among friends by the most reverberating grunts and squeals. She was too big to dislodge, so a tin plate was beaten with a spoon outside and assuming dinner was ready, Muriel would waddle quickly out of the church.

Found in the jungle as an orphan wild piglet, Muriel was reared on a baby's bottle. When the time came for the regiment to move on to Belgaum, she weighed 400 lbs, was housetrained and slept on the verandah of the company bungalow. When the company tried to include her under the heading 'horses and mules', the brigade would not wear this, and said a pig couldn't travel at the Government's expense. Muriel was therefore smuggled onto the train in a crate, with the twenty soldiers needed to load her whistling and singing to conceal the infuriated grunts and squeals of the outraged pig.

Muriel loved Belgaum, and as an early jogger joined the company cross-country runs, usually coming fifth or sixth out of 200 runners. Sometimes the company did a demonstration of a bayonet charge, and Muriel always went in with the assault wave, adding her squeals to the general din.

Sadly, concludes the Inniskilling Journal, when the Battalion left for Iraq in 1924, Muriel was given to some Gunners. Word later reached the stunned and outraged battalion that the perfidious gunners had killed Muriel and eaten her for Christmas.

An equally sad fate awaited Denis, another pig and one of the sole survivors of the German cruiser *Dresden*. When *Dresden* was sunk by *H.M.S. Kent* and *H.M.S. Glasgow* off Juan Fernandez Island during World War I, British sailors dived to the pig's rescue. He was subsequently rescued and rechristened Tirpitz, became the mascot of *H.M.S. Glasgow*, and was decorated with an Iron Cross for standing by his sinking ship. After many months at sea, like many other mascots who outgrew their lovability, Tirpitz was sent to Whale Island Zoo. Even his stay here was ignominiously cut short by the butcher. In 1919, in the guise of pork, he raised £1,785 at a Red Cross auction.

One animal who constantly defied authority and court martial was Charles the Monk, a small grey African monkey, mascot of 311 Battery 73 Heavy A.A. Regiment. Every morning, Charles dropped in on the battery major to watch him shave, and drink his shaving water. On one occasion he broke up the major's tent and, finding a letter addressed to the major's wife, opened it, leaving the envelope behind, and removed the letter to read at his leisure. On another occasion he spent a joyous afternoon in the officer's mess smashing all the china. Even worse, he broke into a nearby Italian cottage and smashed all the religious paintings on the walls.

Among Charles's other vices were smoking and drinking. He was always stealing cigarettes, and on one occasion was discovered in front of a mirror with one in his mouth, fumbling with a box of matches. He also frequented the local cafe, and often left very much worse for wear, staggering along on three legs and passing out on the way home.

It is a lamentable fact that many mascots seem to have taken to the bottle. The Seaforth Highlanders, for example, had a baby elephant in Edinburgh, who plunged his trunk into the numerous pots of beer that were offered him, until keeper and mascot would totter home to his stable in a drunken stupor. Equally Tirah, the donkey mascot of the King's Own Yorkshire Light Infantry in India, developed a taste for beer, and after a drinking bout would stagger off, find a bungalow and sleep it off on one of the soldier's beds, usually after it had been tidied up for inspection. Tirah's drink problem became so serious he was banned to the horse lines. Drying out made him so irritable that when the regiment moved on he was left behind.

Saddest perhaps of all the mascots was Donald the drunken deer, who was attached to the 42nd Royal Highlanders in the 1830s. Donald developed a very insidious passion for sherry and whiskey, and used to make his way nightly to the men's rooms touting for tots. His hangovers were so frightful the next day that he started butting everyone who crossed the square. As his antlers grew, his behaviour deteriorated, and when the regiment was posted to Corfu it was felt they could not take Donald, so Lord Bandon offered him the run of his fine park in Bandon Castle.

'It was really an affecting sight,' writes Major Edwards in *Mascots and Pets of the Services*, 'to see poor Donald thrown over, and tied with rope by those he loved so well, and put into a cart to be carried off. His cries were so pitiful, he actually shed tears, and so did some of his friends.'

When he reached Bandon Castle, Donald became a recluse, attacking anyone who came near him. There were so many complaints that he finally had to be shot. Poor Donald, like so many mascots, 'his regiment and his soldier comrades were the only home he knew, and his happiness left him when he was separated.'

Donald's career was not unlike that of Beauty, the big black Alsatian bitch who became the mascot of the W.A.A.F. She moved with her unit to many stations in England, guarding the camp, collecting the post, and making friends with the camp cat on each occasion. When the regiment split up, one of the girls took her home, but it was a long time before she settled down to civilian life. She missed the W.A.A.Fs desperately, and whenever she saw one in uniform would give a bark of joy and rush up and try to kiss her.

Unlike the mine dogs and guard dogs, who were loaned by their owners, and who had experienced a happy civilian life before the war, a military life was the only one most of the mascots knew. When they were demobbed and sent to zoos or even private homes, they missed the excitement, the admiration, and loving attention of lots of different people. As Margot Asquith so wisely pointed out in her *Autobiography* 'If you have been sunned through and through like an apricot on a wall . . . you are oversensitive to any withdrawal of heat.'

Happiest perhaps was the fate of Bud, a brindled bull terrier, smuggled into France when he was five weeks old by Mr 'Slats' Slattery of the 82nd Division, 325th Machine Gun Company. Bud was gassed in the Argonne, and subsequently wore a special gas mask, took part in a big engagement on the Somme, and learnt to flatten with the men when the shells came over. He just escaped death, while begging for food, when the division kitchen was shelled and the cook and all the kitchen hands killed. But he survived and managed to fight alongside the same master, Mr Slattery, throughout the war, returned home to America with him, and lived to a fine age of thirteen.

When he died, his heartbroken master wrapped Bud in his old campaign rug, placed him in a rough pine box, and took him to a nearby war cemetery. While he was digging the grave, one of the cemetery staff strolled up and, sensing the ex-soldier's desolation, unearthed an old rusty bugle. As Bud was lowered into the grave, the last post rang out.

Venus, a sea-dog (bitch?), was a British destroyer captain's mascot during World War II. IWM

The Hall of Fame

Bobby of Maiwand

Bobby, a white mongrel, was attached to the 2nd Battalion, the Royal Berkshire Regiment, with whom he went to India when the Afghan War broke out. He was present at the famous Battle of Maiwand in 1880 when the British were overwhelmed by an enemy ten times their number. His battalion was gradually whittled down, until they were all killed and only Bobby, who'd stood barking defiantly at the head of

LC

the gallant little band throughout the engagement, was left. Taken prisoner, he later joined the remnants of the regiment, at Kandahar. Back in England, Bobby, wearing a smart scarlet coat trimmed with fake pearls, was presented to Queen Victoria. She listened to his story with rapt attention, begged to see his back where he'd been wounded, and pinned the Afghan Medal on his collar. After being taken up by royalty, Bobby became very much above himself, and refused to fraternise with any of the local dogs. Nemesis descended in the form of a hansom cab which ran him over in Gosport. Queen Victoria is said to have cried when she heard this sad news.

Prince – the miracle finder

Prince, an Irish Terrier, was devoted to his master, Private James Brown of the North Staffordshire Regiment, and was quite inconsolable when Mr Brown was posted to France in September 1914. Then one day he disappeared from his home in Hammersmith, and to everyone's amazement turned up at Armentières a few weeks later, and tracked down his master in the trenches in a frenzy of delight. Because no one could believe the story, the Commanding Officer had master and dog paraded in front of him next morning. Evidently Prince had cunningly attached himself to some troops who were crossing the Channel, and by some sixth sense had managed to locate his master. He became the hero of the regiment, and fought beside his master for the rest of the war.

Simon – the champion ratter

Simon, a handsome black and white cat, belonged to the captain of *H.M.S. Amethyst*, and was given to

strolling across the knees of his master's guests at dinner, and sitting on the chart whenever a course was being laid. On 20 April 1949 Simon was thrust into war, when Chinese Communist batteries opened fire on his ship in the Yangtze river. A shell landed on the captain's cabin, killing his master, wounding Simon in several places, and singeing his fur and whiskers. For a few days he took refuge, but the shelling had shaken numerous rats out of their normal hiding place. Simon therefore left the comfort of the captain's cabin, and lodged in the Petty Officer's mess to be nearer the scene of operations and to make his raid on the rats. His catches were so numerous that they were recorded on a list. When the ship escaped on 31 July, Simon carried on ratting. News of his heroism preceded him, and when the crippled *Amethyst* limped into Hong Kong, numerous letters, telegrams, tins of food, and cheques to buy cream awaited him. Sadly, in quarantine, he missed his ship mates so much, he pined away and died, but was later awarded a 'Pussthumous' Dickin Medal.

Daisy – the dog comforter

Daisy was the mascot mongrel of a Norwegian trawler which was torpedoed by the enemy. Those of the crew not killed outright were thrown into an icy sea. Daisy went with them, and through the dark chill hours of night, swam from one man to another, licking their faces, as though seeking to encourage and comfort them. When they were at last picked up and landed in Britain, all the crew were unanimous in their praise of Daisy, who they said had put new hope into them. As a result of her unselfish heroism, Daisy was awarded a medal by the R.S.P.C.A.

Peggy – the dog saviour

Peggy, a mongrel, was awarded an inscribed collar by the R.S.P.C.A. When her house was bombed, her mistress was trapped under the debris, and the baby in the pram was almost suffocated by a fall of plaster. Peggy who could have bolted through the window, sat on top of the pram, working furiously with her little paws, until she made a hole big enough for the baby to breathe through. She then sat down, and waited for the rescuers. One false move could have brought a fresh fall of rubble on both the baby and herself, but in the end, mother, child, and dog were saved.

Antis – the air ace

When Czech air gunner Jan Bozdech was shot down during a raid over Germany, he rescued a starving Alsatian puppy from a bombed-out farm house and smuggled him back across the French lines. As France fell, Jan made his way South carrying the dog, now called Antis and almost full grown, most of the way. Trying to escape to Algiers, their plane was shot down over the sea. Jan, swimming with Antis clinging to his back, was finally rescued by an Italian convoy, only to

Lord Wavell presents Antis with his Dickin Medal, having addressed his speech of congratulation to the dog personally. Antis was so intelligent that he probably understood every word.

be sunk by a British warship and rescued again. In England, Jan joined the R.A.F. Such was Antis's devotion to his master by this time, that he soon stowed away on Jan's flights. Twice wounded, once very badly in the face, the dog lay quietly in a pool of his own blood at his master's feet, until the plane returned to base four hours later.

Antis also rescued many casualties from bombed buildings, and repeatedly disputed the evidence of the All Clear by warning his master that enemy planes were still in the area. After the war, man and dog returned to Czechoslovakia, but soon fell foul of the Communist authorities. Leaving a family he loved, with only Antis for comfort and protection, Jan made the deadly journey through the Iron Curtain. Antis continually warned him of enemy patrols, and saved Jan's life by attacking and pinning down a border guard. Back in London, in 1949, Antis became the first foreign dog to win the Dickin Medal.

Judy – the prisoner of war

Judy, the mascot of several ships in the Pacific, was captured by the Japanese in 1942, and interned in a prison camp at Medan. Here she met Leading Aircraftsman Frank Williams, who shared his small helping of rice with her, and won her love and loyalty for life. Judy raised morale in the P.O.W. camp, giving the alarm when crocodiles, poisonous snakes, and even tigers approached. Falling foul of the camp commandant, she was smuggled out in a rice sack, when the prisoners were shipped back to Singapore. For three hours she lay upside down in the sack in the blazing tropical sun, never whimpering, moving or betraying her presence to the Japanese guard.

Next day the ship was torpedoed and Judy was separated from her master. Three days later, on the way to another prison camp, they met again, and their reunion was described by an officer as joyous and touching. Finally they ended up at a camp with the same Japanese commandant they'd outwitted at Medan, who condemned Judy to death, and ordered the prisoners to eat her as a punishment. Fortunately she went into hiding, and the Japs by this time were too terrified of reprisals to carry out the threat. The highlights of Judy's P.O.W. life were having nine puppies and finding an elephant's shinbone, which took her two hours to bury.

Smuggled back to England on a troop ship, Judy

Judy wearing the Dickin Medal and its ribbon. IWM

emerged from quarantine in a blaze of glory. She was awarded the Dickin Medal, and her bark was heard on the B.B.C.

Rifleman Khan

An outstandingly courageous Alsatian attached to the 6th Battalion of the Cameronians, Khan was devoted to his handler, Corporal J. Muldoon. Both took part in the assault on the Dutch Island of Walcheren in 1944 – one of the fiercest engagements of the war. Muldoon

IWM

and Khan were approaching Walcheren, under heavy shellfire, when their boat capsized. Khan set out calmly for the shore, and on arrival looked anxiously round for his master, but found him nowhere to be seen. Unlike Khan, Muldoon couldn't swim. Hearing his cries for help over the noise of the battle, Khan ignored the falling shells and plunged back into the sea. After a desperate search he found a drowning Muldoon, who had just enough strength left to cling onto the dog and be towed back to shore. For this gallant, loyal and faithful action, Khan was awarded a Dickin Medal.

Rats – the dog soldier

Easily, the most famous of postwar mascots, Rats, the jaunty little mongrel, adored soldiers and for many years attached himself to different British army units in Crossmaglen, one of the most threatened Northern Ireland trouble spots.

Serving with the Grenadier Guards, the Marines, the Queen's Own Highlanders, and the Welsh Guards, Rats went on ceaseless patrols, car chases and helicopter flights, when he gave everyone heart attacks, leaping thirty feet to the ground, as the helicopter came down to land.

He was shot at more times than anyone could remember; he was blown up by bombs including a firebomb, which burnt several inches off his tail. Four pieces of metal lay trapped along his spine; shotgun pellets still lodged in his chest; he was run over twice by cars in the course of duties, leaving him with permanently bent paws. Worst of all, being such an affectionate dog, he had to suffer the heartbreak of losing a beloved master and finding a new one each time a unit moved on.

Gradually his fame spread, and he became not only an I.R.A. hit target, but also a national celebrity, receiving two sacks of mail a day, which took six fulltime soldiers to answer. He was also given numerous presents from admirers including one old lady who sent him last week's copy of the *Radio Times* and *T.V. Times* each week.

His greatest service to the army, however, was boosting morale. 'At the head of the patrol, half strutting, half waddling briskly and happily ahead, he gave the illusion that all was right with the world and death and violence merely a bad dream.'

Or as another soldier who served with him said, 'Rats was oasis of friendship, in a desert of sadness.'

Finally in 1980 the exertions of war took their toll on his small frame. On doctor's orders, he was given an honourable retirement, and a very distinguished passing-out parade. Now he lives happily in Kent, where new hobbies include chasing the local pheasants.

Rats, the dog soldier. MOD

All Creatures Great and Small

He prayeth best who loveth best
All things both great and small
For the dear God who loveth us
He made and loveth all.

SAMUEL TAYLOR COLERIDGE: *The Ancient Mariner*

The donkey is such an endearing, comical creature that few people realise how stoically he has served in war. Who today remembers the East African campaign of 1916–17, described as a 'veritable chamber of horrors', in which thousands and thousands of donkeys died a terrible death from tsetse flies. After the campaign was over, one of the captured German veterinary officers admitted that their Commander-in-Chief, General Von Lettow, had kept his veterinary services wholly employed in surveying the country so that he could base his retreat on the areas reported most deadly to animal life. When the area was unsuitable for his whole army to occupy, he would send a strong force of infantry into this deadly country, knowing the British would soon pursue it into the area.

In one instance between August and October 1916, General Von Lettow retreated along a road between Korogwe to Morogoro into the tsetse fly area, and a British mounted brigade, consisting of 4,000 horses and donkeys, was soon hot on his heels. Within three weeks, the entire 4,000 were dead. Whereupon 8,000 donkey and horse reinforcements were sent along the same route, and in the same way every single one dropped dead.

Even worse, like some dreadful Agatha Christie nightmare, was the cure. Donkeys and other animals were given small doses of arsenic every day to mitigate the effect of the tsetse fly, enabling them to stagger on, despite being infected, for another six weeks. Two and a half million tablets were issued for this purpose, so the animals could be kept at work till they dropped. The tablets were supposed to be crushed up and sprinkled on each animal's food, but this was too much like hard work for many of the grooms and drivers. Instead they dropped the tablets into the nosebag, where, uneaten, they sank to the bottom. Proof of this was tragically provided on one occasion, when an officer ordered the leftovers from the nosebags to be collected together and given to some late arrivals. These unfortunate donkeys died immediately from massive doses of arsenic. Out of 34,000 donkeys employed during the campaign, only 1,042 were still alive at the end. Horses and mules died in equally

Though they started off their career on horses, the Blues have used many means of locomotion since. During the troubles in Cyprus, while normally mounted in armoured cars, they did not disdain the humble donkey.
CENTRAL OFFICE OF INFORMATION

appalling numbers, and 120,000 Africans had to be brought in to lug the guns, and carry the dead animals' packs.

More donkeys served on the Western Front during the First World War. E.H. Baynes, in *Animal Heroes of the Great War*, tells the poignant tale of a British officer meeting a convoy of French donkeys carrying supplies up to the trenches. Suddenly he noticed that the smallest donkey had no ears. The driver explained that a shell had exploded in its face, cutting off its ears, and blinding the poor little fellow at the same time. The officer, deeply moved, ran his hand over the pathetic furry face saying, 'Oh you plucky little devil, you certainly deserve the Croix de Guerre.'

In France, donkeys carried panniers up to the front, often staggering under bulky 200-lb loads out of all proportion to their size. Tended by soldiers who were considered too old to fight, the donkeys were small enough to be led along the trenches to distribute rations. Sometimes when it was bitterly cold, men took them into the dugouts to cuddle them at night. They were probably too exhausted to mind the fact that donkeys are great dreamers and kick like mad in their sleep.

Donkeys also served gallantly at Gallipoli – where, like animated scrap heaps, they staggered up the beach weighed down by so many water cans, you could hardly see the little animal underneath. A number of donkeys with Greek drivers were landed in April 1915, also to carry water; but their drivers were soon deported and the donkeys left to get in the way and graze idly in the gullies until they disappeared. One of these donkeys, however, was destined for immortality. Like many legends, he has several names – Duffy, Murphy, and Abdul being among them.

We do, however, know the name of his master: John Simpson, an Englishman who emigrated to Australia and enlisted in the 3rd Australian Field Ambulance Corps. Passionately fond of animals – every dog in camp was his friend – Simpson even managed to take a young possum with him on the trip to Europe.

At Gallipoli, he was the second man ashore from his boat, but the first and third, stretcher bearers like himself, were both killed. So heavy were the casualties among bearers, and so extensive the loss of medical equipment, that suddenly, entirely on his own initiative, Private Simpson set himself up as a one man Red Cross Service. Seeing Duffy/Murphy/Abdul grazing lazily nearby, he made friends with the little donkey and enlisted his help.

For the next twenty-five days and nights, Simpson and Duffy toiled together, bringing comfort to the dying and first aid to those with minor injuries, but above all, carrying any soldier who had enough strength to cling onto a donkey out of the firing line back to the safety of the beach ambulance stations. The fighting was too furious for anyone to count how many hundreds of lives they saved, as back and forth man and donkey travelled across the valley of death. Seemingly oblivious of the constant shelling and deadly sniping, trusting in one another so utterly, they appeared to bear a charmed life.

Each night, Simpson snatched a brief rest, sleeping beside Duffy in the Indian mule lines, but the little donkey was always ready to go back to the firing line when his master asked. Such was their success that Simpson commandeered another donkey. On 19 May, he went up the valley past the water guard, where he generally had his breakfast. That day it wasn't ready.

'Never mind,' called Simpson cheerfully, 'I'll have a good dinner instead when we come back.'

They never did. Supporting two patients on his donkey team, he was climbing slowly down the creek bed, when a shell killed both him and the donkeys. Both their patients survived, and Private Simpson and Duffy had by their gallantry won their way into every Australian history book.

When the supply of camels ran out in Palestine towards the end of 1917, 12,790 donkey reinforcements were brought in from Egypt. According to the official Veterinary Corps history, 'They were an excellent lot of animals, remarkably uniform in size, free from lameness and vice, who repeatedly proved their worth during operations in the Judean Hills.' Initially the cold upset them dreadfully, and 233 donkeys died from exposure; but courageously the rest soon became acclimatised, and with packs on their backs helped

Allenby build his roads along the front from Jaffa to Jerusalem and brought supplies of jam, biscuits and bully beef up to the troops.

Their finest hour in Palestine came on 1 May 1918, when British troops were desperately struggling to defend Es Salt. Ammunition and food had nearly run out, and fresh supplies had to be sent up before morning. No vehicle could possibly get up the mountain track, and the journey had to be made at night, so noisy camels were quite out of the question. Each of the cavalry regiments had a few donkeys used by cooks and batmen. About 200 were loaded up with ammunition and food. Marching all night, they reached Es Salt, which was being hotly attacked by the enemy, delivered their sorely needed ammunition saved the day, and returned to safety. The distance covered was forty miles over appalling country, and in constant danger of running into the enemy.

Even in the midst of battle, animals often seem to make the most of situations. Tiny the donkey, found dying by the roadside in Salonika, is clearly enjoying herself drinking tea with the 26th Dvisional Train. She subsequently became their mascot. IWM

Nor should it be forgotten that the Italians employed no fewer than 100,000 donkeys in World War I, requisitioned from peasant farmers. They worked in the mountains, and were quartered in barracks heated in winter by little stoves. E.H. Baynes tells of one hilarious occasion in the Alps, when a donkey train carrying ammunition arrived at one of the peaks. At precisely the same moment, the Austrians opened fire with an intensive bombardment, whereupon the startled donkeys trotted towards the enemy and began to bray in chorus. It sounded so like contemptuous laughter that the Italians threw their hats in the air and cheered.

Bullocks reluctantly enter an aircraft preparatory to being flown to base behind the Japanese lines in northern Burma, to provide additional transport for the Chindits. IWM

Fortunately, in World War II, the donkey was largely supplanted as a beast of burden by his offspring the mule; but he often turned up as a spoilt, adored mascot. In fact Barney, a donkey foal won by the R.A.F. in a darts match against the Navy, was the first mascot to be registered in the Allied Forces Mascot Club run by the P.D.S.A.

Even today, like some wiry old territorial officer, the donkey is often recalled to service. In 1973, when the British were fighting Arab guerrillas in Oman, parties of donkeys, their feet muffled with hessian, were taken up into the mountains in four-ton lorries, until the lorries could go no further and the donkeys were unloaded to carry vital ammunition and supplies over the steep mountain tracks.

A Royal Engineer commando, who went on a mountaineering exercise in Nepal in 1981, told me that they took four horses and a donkey who completely ruled the party, keeping all four horses in order. He also sulked terribly if he had to march at the back, constantly waiting for an opportunity to nip through when no one was looking and take the lead. Once in front he set a cracking pace, encouraging the horses to follow him up steep places they would never have normally dared to tackle, carrying on until everyone in the party was dropping with exhaustion.

The ox, that other unlauded beast of burden, shares with the donkey a place in the stable when the Prince of Peace was born. It is a fitting reward for the great courage, industry and stoical acceptance of his lot that he has shown in war. As was pointed out in the chapter on the elephant, it was the twenty strong teams of oxen, who took over and dragged the heavy seige guns up to the firing line when the elephant was too scared to go any nearer. Over and over again, in Germany, India, Mesopotamia, when motor transport got bogged down the despised ox with his titanic strength saved the situation. During the British occupation of Baghdad in 1917, when it was 122° in the shade, oxen were the backbone of the transport, and died agonisingly from sunstroke. In the East African campaign, ox transport was largely depended on, but no line of retreat could be called safe for cattle. Deadly diseases lurked everywhere: rinderpest, the tsetse fly, not to mention the terrible ticks, the predatory tick birds and cow herons who eat the ticks, then prey on the sores left behind. Yet over the worst kind of roads, through bush that seemed impenetrable, in the suffocating heat of the jungle, the patient oxen hauled until they dropped.

In Italy, where they pulled big guns, they were kept in camps near the river, where they could bathe and

When words failed, U.S. Marines used physical persuasion to induce an ox to move up war supplies to front lines on the island of Saipon, where organised Japanese resistance ended on 8 July 1944.

Even reindeer were used as transport in northern Russia late in 1918-19. IWM

water in peace, were washed with damp straw, and existed on grass, hay, and a little corn if the work was really heavy. A touching characteristic of the ox is that he develops a decided affection for his teammates, and hates being split up from them. He would endure cannonfire most bravely, but got terribly upset if he saw any other oxen lying dead in the road, and refused to go on working. When he was wounded he was also incredibly stoical, and made the perfect patient in the Blue Cross hospitals.

In World War II, oxen were again called up in the East, in Germany and in the Red Army to pull the heavy guns, while in Finland, even the timid reindeer was conscripted into service to drag supplies over the snow. Nor should we forget the thousands of animals who die needlessly, it often seems, when the military authorities get together with scientists. During World War II when the British were panicking about the effects of chemical warfare, 15,000–20,000 monkeys, dogs, cats, rabbits, guinea pigs, rats and pigeons were collected in two farms to test the effects of poison gas. Live animals including pigs and dogs were also left for hours alone on warships before being blown to smithereens in atom bomb tests, and millions of animals throughout the world at this very moment are suffering fearful pain in laboratories as scientists test the effects of radiation burns.

The scientist works on the premise that any crime is

worth committing on an animal, if there is even a faint possibility this might save a human life. But surely this doesn't justify the work of a Harvard Professor, Dr Louis Feiser, who during World War II hatched a plot to bombard the Japs with bats equipped with tiny incendiary bombs, which would trigger off a thousand fires.

According to Robert Lubow, in his fascinating book *The War Animals*, the bombs were attached by surgery with a piece of string through the bats' chests. The plan was to drop them over large Japanese cities. On landing, the bats were expected to find a hiding place then, irritated by the string, chew through it, leaving the tiny bombs to explode. After two years' research, a trial run was made in New Mexico. The results were straight out of *M.A.S.H.* On the first day, several bats escaped and set off fires which completely demolished a general's car and a million-pound hangar. The poor bats were then chilled in a cold room, to force them prematurely into hibernation, and dropped again in New Mexico, where they were expected to wake up at a certain altitude on reaching the warm lower air over the desert. Sadly, the majority slept on and crashed to their deaths. By this time it was 1944, and the grisly project was scrapped.

Extensive tests have also been carried out in America to see if wild animals can detect the presence of enemy intruders in the jungle. Again in *The War Animals*, Robert Lubow describes two hilarious experiments. The first took place in Panama, where the Americans 'created jungle conditions in a heavily vegetated island in the Panama Canal,' into which they fed 56 animals, 306 birds, 62 snakes, and 33 crocodiles and lizards – rather like some ghastly cocktail party. They then recorded the jungle sounds, first when no human was present, secondly when two intruders passed through, and finally when two intruders stopped for a couple of hours. Thirty different animal noises were analysed including three frogs, a howler monkey and a fulvous-bellied ant-wren. At the end of this extremely costly experiment, the momentous conclusion was reached that 'most birds indicate the presence of people by decreasing their rate of vocalisation,' which when translated into English means they sang less.

Even more ludicrously, in 1963 the U.S. Army tried to train guard bugs to detect ambushes and enemy intruders. If a mosquito or flea can find a man easily, the army reasoned, could he not be trained to report these findings back to base. Eventually tests were made on the giant cone nose bug, the bedbug, lice, the oriental rat flea, the tick and the mosquito. The procedure was for a human being to breathe on the various insects, then the noise of their reactions was to be recorded.

Lice evidently were useless, because they didn't show any excitement at all during the tests, and apparently only stumbled on humans by mistake. The oriental rat flea exhibited violent jumping when breathed on, making a sound like popping corn, but he took a long time to calm down, and couldn't go without food for long enough. Ticks were excellent; they could survive for hours on end without a bite of human to eat, and went from complete stillness to violent activity, but they moved so quietly that no sound was recorded. Experiments to put shoes on their tiny feet proved a conspicuous failure.

In the end, six cone nose bugs were used in a field test on twelve humans. The humans formed into ambushes of four and hid along the road. The experiment wasn't a wild success, because although the cone nose bugs became frightfully excited every time they passed an ambush, no doubt stimulated by their unexpected trip outside, they also became frightfully excited by everything else as well. However, the Americans are persisting with such experiments, and the guard bug may well become a deterrent of the future.

Scientists all over the world have also for many years been experimenting with dolphins. Again according to Mr Lubow, when a pregnant dolphin is about to give birth, two girlfriend dolphins trail her everywhere and, the moment her baby is born, they lift it gently to the surface to give it its first breath of air. Other dolphins evidently perform the same service to any dolphin who is ill. It seems sad that these larky, unselfish, intensely gregarious creatures should be dragged into our conflicts. But, alas, they are far too intelligent to be left out. Anything a dog does on land,

Port Elizabeth, South Africa: the memorial to the 326,073 horses who died in the Boer War, and to all animals who have perished through human conflicts.

a dolphin can do in the sea. Like the Russian suicide dog, he can carry detonated explosive down to an enemy ship and blow it and himself up; he can guard harbours against enemy frogmen and submarines; he can glide through the most elaborate burglar alarm systems and security nets, carrying electronic listening devices to enemy ships to test the efficiency of their defence. Most vital of all, perhaps, he can locate and retrieve bombs from the sea.

In April 1976, *Newsday Magazine* published an interview with a former American army scientist, in which he said the Navy and the C.I.A. used dolphins to retrieve a nuclear bomb which had fallen into the sea from a Navy plane flying near Puerto Rico.

Both dolphins and sealions, in fact, have been taught to dive down with recovery grabbers attached to their muzzles. These consist of telescopic arms which lock round the bomb so it can be lifted up to the surface. In one American test, one is glad to learn that one dolphin deserted and joined a passing shoal, while a sealion surfaced with a mouthful of squid, and enjoyed it so much that he dived back under and was never seen again.

Dolphins, in fact, have become such invaluable allies that a few years ago, Russia made a law that they were no longer to be butchered for food (a huge industry in that country), because they were all needed for biological research. More recently both pilot and killer whales have been trained to find and recover metal cylinders from the seabed. Soon no doubt their skills will become so useful that a conservation order will be slapped on them, too, and the army ironically will have succeeded where Greenpeace has failed. But recently, during the Falklands War, the British torpedoed three unfortunate whales, believing them to be enemy submarines.

Occasionally one is delighted to hear of animals getting their own back. In Africa in World War I, lions charged the lines and held General Smuts prisoner in his car; giraffes smashed down telephone wires, elephants smashed the poles, rhinoceros butted into camps and marching troops; and a swarm of bees attacked a transport column and brought the British army temporarily to a standstill.

Evidently, too, when a British officer crashed his car in a bog, he had an awful time, dodging wild boar, leopard, crocodile, and hippos. During a three-day struggle back to civilisation, having swum seven rivers, he sank exhausted at the foot of a tree. When he came to he found two baboons quarrelling over his trousers, now in shreds among the top branches of a forty-foot tree.

In a strange role reversal too of the Ancient Mariner, albatrosses evidently attacked sailors drowning off the Falkland Islands, and in the Pacific, sharks usually clean up the human debris after a ship had been blown up.

But it is a miniscule return for what humans have done to animals. The Lord God may have made All Creatures Great and Small, but Man has consistently exploited them, and allowed them to be slaughtered in their millions, to satisfy his lust to dominate his fellow men.

There is not a member of the animal kingdom who has not been affected at some time by war, from the thousands of fish lying stunned or dead on top of the water after every naval battle to the sheepdogs in the Falklands today, who are desperately worried because their flocks have been scattered by the Argentine Army, and are now in constant danger from Argentinian mines. Even the little glowworm has come to our aid. In the First World War, an officer would walk ahead carrying one to guide tanks, secretly taking up a position the night before an action.

Most animals who died have no memorial. Sick, wounded, starved, slaughtered, they have perished as though they had never been. The only way we can repay them is to treat them with more kindness in peace, and hope that in the future they are drawn as little as possible into our wars.

Surely their best memorial was provided by the South Africans after the Boer War. A beautiful statue, it stands in Port Elizabeth, and shows a kneeling soldier giving water to his horse. Underneath are the words:

'The greatness of a nation consists not so much in the numbers of its people, or the extent of its territory – as in the extent and justice of its compassion.'

Bibliography

AMBRUS, V.G. *Horses in Battle* (London: Oxford University Press)

ANGLESEY, The Marquess of. *A History of the British Cavalry 1816–1919 Volume I 1816–1850* (London: Leo Cooper)

ANGLESEY, The Marquess of. *A History of the British Cavalry 1816–1919 Volume III 1872–1898* (London: Leo Cooper/ Secker & Warburg)

BAKER, P. Shaw. *Animal War Heroes* (London: A & C Black)

BANKS, A. *A World of Military History Volume I to 1500* (London: Seeley Service)

BARTLETT, H. Moyse. *Louis Edward Nolan and his Influence on the British Cavalry* (London: Leo Cooper)

BARZILAY, D. *The British Army in Ulster Volume II* (London: Century Services Ltd)

BAYNES, E.H. *Animal Heroes of the Great War* (London: Macmillan)

BLENKINSOP, Major General Sir L.J. and Lt.-Col. J.W. Rainey. *Official History of the War Veterinary Services*

BRERETON, J.M. *The Horse in War* (Newton Abbot: David & Charles)

CLABBY, J. *The History of the Royal Army Veterinary Corps 1919–1961* (J.A. Allen)

COOPER, L. *British Regular Cavalry 1644–1914* (Chapman & Hall)

EDWARDS, Major T.J. *Mascots and Pets of the Services* (Gale & Polden)

FAIRHOLME, and PAIN, W. *A Century of Work for Animals* (London: John Murray)

FITZGERALD, B. Vesey. *The Book of the Dog* (Nicholson & Watson)

FITZGERALD, B. Vesey. *The Book of the Horse* (Nicholson & Watson)

GALTREY, S. *The Horse and the War* (London: Country Life)

GARNETT, D. (Ed.) *The Letters of T.E. Lawrence* (London: Jonathan Cape)

GLADSTONE, H. *Birds and the War* (Skeffington)

HALSTOCK, M. *Rats: The Story of a Dog Soldier* (London: Gollancz)

HAMMERTON, J.A. *The War Illustrated Volume III* (Amalgamated Press Ltd)

INCHBALD, G. *Imperial Camel Corps* (Johnson)

LEWIN, R. *Slim: The Standardbearer* (London: Leo Cooper)

LUBOW, R.E. *The War Animals, The Training and Use of Animals as Weapons of War* (New York: Doubleday)

MARWICK, A. *Women at War 1914–1918* (London: Fontana)

MITCHELL, E. *Light Horse, The Story of Australia's Mounted Troops* (Macmillan)

MORGAN, G. *Soldier Bear* (London/Glasgow: Collins)

MOSS, A.W. and KIRBY, E. *Valiant Crusade: A History of the R.S.P.C.A.* (London: Cassell)

MOTTISTONE, Lord. *My Horse Warrior* (London: Hodder & Stoughton)

OSMAN, Lt.-Col. A.H. *Pigeons in the Great War* (The Racing Pigeon)

OSMAN, Major W.H. *Pigeons in World War II* (The Racing Pigeon)

RICHARDSON, A. *One Man and His Dog* (London: Harrap)

RICHARDSON, Lt.-Col. E.H. *Forty Years With Dogs* (London: Hutchinson)

RICHARDSON, Lt.-Col. E.H. *British War Dogs* (Skeffington)

RICHARDSON, Lt.-Col. E.H. and Mrs. *Fifty Years With Dogs* (London: Hutchinson)

ROGERS, Lt.-Col. H.C.B. *The Mounted Troops of the British Army* (London: Seeley Service)

ST HILL BOURNE, D. *They Also Serve* (Winchester Publications)

TAMBLYN, Lt.-Col. D.S. *The Horse in War* (The Jackson Press)

TERRAINE, J. *The Smoke and the Fire: Myths and Anti-Myths of War 1861–1945* (London: Sidgwick & Jackson)

THOMSON, J.R. Fawcett. *The Animals Go Too* (Gawthorn)

TREW, C.G. *The Story of the Dog* (London: Methuen)

WILLIAMS, J.H. *Elephant Bill* (London: Rupert Hart-Davis/ The Reprint Society)

Index

Page references in *italics* are to illustrations.
Animals' names are also printed in *italics*.

Afghan War, use of camels, 84, *86*
Albert, Prince Consort, *21*
Alexander the Great, *14*, 15
Allenby, General Edmund, 45, 87, 91, 134, 157
Alsatian dogs, *64*, 65
American Civil War, new cavalry tactics in, 23
Ammunition-carrying dogs, 63, *63*, 64
Andrew (cat mascot of Mascot Club), *140*
Anglesey, George Charles Henry Victor Paget, 7th Marquess of, 23, 84, 87
'Animals' V.C.', *see* Dickin Medal
Antis (dog), 150–1, *150*
Armour
  for horses, 16
  introduced into Britain, 16
Army Veterinary Corps
  foundation, 27
  purchases camels, 88
  role in World War I, 36, *38*, 39
  see also Royal Army Veterinary Corps
Army War Dog School, 64
Artillery, as backing for cavalry, 19
Asquith, Margot, 146
Attila the Hun, 15
Australian Walers (horses), 24–5
Aylward, Sergeant-Major, 71

Balkans Campaign, 96
Bamse (dog mascot, Norwegian Navy ship *Thorod*), 137–8, *137*
Bandit (Household Cavalry horse), 53
Bandon, Lord, 146
Bandoola (elephant), 117, 119
Bannockburn, Battle of (1314), 16
Barney (donkey mascot), 158
Barrow, Major-General Sir George, 47
Bayeux Tapestry, 16, *17*
Baynes, E.H., 87, 88, 156, 158
Beauty (Alsatian mascot, W.A.A.F.), 146
Beauty (P.D.S.A. dog mascot), 124, *125*, *127*
Beersheba, Battle of (1917), 45
Beresford, Lord Charles, 87
Beresford, Captain Lord Patrick, 86
Billy (dog mascot, Royal Ulster Rifles), 137
Bimbashi (camel), 86
Bing (dog mascot, Parachute Regiment), 67, 69
Birds
  feeding in wartime, 130
  ornithology in war, 134, 136
Blondi (Hitler's Alsatian), 134
Blue Cross, activities in World War I, 42
Blues and Royals Mounted Squadron, 12
Bob (patrol dog), 67
Bobbie (antelope mascot, Royal Warwickshire Regiment), 143, *143*
Bobby (dog mascot, Royal Berkshire Regiment), 148, *148*
Boer War
  Australian Walers (horses), 24–5
  horses, *24*, *25*, *26*
    casualty figures, 27
    for food in sieges, 27
    memorial, *162*, 163
  mascots, 136–7
  tactics of Boer farmers, 23–4
  use of ox teams, *22*
Bombing, Hyde Park nail bomb (1982), 12, *13*
Boy (dog mascot, Cavaliers), 134
Bozdech, Jan, 150–1
Bradley, J.B., 119
Brereton, J.M., 18, 20, 34, 43, 45, 51
Brooke, Dorothy, 48–9, *48*
Bruno (bear mascot, H.M.S. *Aboukir*), 140
Bucephalus (Alexander the Great's horse), *14*, 15
Bud (bull terrier mascot, 325th Machine Gun Company), 146
Burma
  use of elephants, 110, *111*, 113, *113*, *114*, 115, *115*
  use of mules, 105, *105*, 106, *106*, *107*, *108*, 109
Burma railway, 119

Calvert, Brigadier M. ('Mad Mike'), 106, 142
Camel Corps, *see* Imperial Camel Corps
Camels, 84–95
  advantages and limitations, 84, 86
  Bactrian and Arabian species, 90–1
  bad habits, 90
  impervious to gunshot noise, 86
  in World War I, 87–95
  in World War II, 87
  omnivorous appetites, 95
  prone to illnesses, 89
Canaries, *82*, 83, *83*
Canine Defence League, 130, 133
  activities in World War II, 121
Cats
  as mascots, 138
  feeding in wartime, 133
  in World War II, 128
Cavalry
  activities in Palestine in World War II, *50*, 51
  backed by artillery, 19
  French, in World War II, 51
  in World War I, 42–3, *43*, 45–6
    Palestine Campaign, 45
  last full-scale charge, 51
  modern-day use in difficult terrain, 51
  regiments mechanised, 49
  role in war, 18
  tactics in American Civil War, 23
Chariots, Egyptian, 13
Charles the Monk (monkey mascot, 73 Heavy A.A. Regiment), 145–6
Charlie (goat mascot, Welsh

Regiment), 145
Charlotte (hen mascot, H.M.S. *Cadmus*), 136
Chauvel, General, 91
Cher Ami (American pigeon), 75
Cheshire Yeomanry, 51
Chlorine gas, 34
  tested on camels, 95
Clabby, J.O., 49, 102
Cox, R.J., 96
Crécy, Battle of (1346), 18
Crimean War, herd instinct of horses demonstrated, 20
Croix de Guerre, awarded to pigeons, 75
Crossbows, 16

Daisy (dog mascot, Norwegian trawler), 149
Darius, King of Persia, 15
Daunt, M.D., 98, 100, 109
Decorations, *see* Croix de Guerre; Dickin Medal; Légion d'Honneur
Dee (dog), 128
Delhi, Battle of (1398), 112
Denis (pig mascot, German ship *Dresden*), 145
Derby VIII (ram mascot, 95th Foot Regiment), 145
Desert foxes, 136
Desert Mounted Corps, 45, 48
Destriers (heavy horses), 16
  rendered obsolete by gunpowder, 18
Dickin Medal, 65, *66*, *67*, 69, 79, *79*, *80*, *81*, 124, 127, *150*, 151, 152
Dodo (guard dog), 71
Dogs, 54–71
  as mascots, 136–8
  best breeds and characteristics, 61, 65
  first British training school, 54, 56–7
  guard duties, 61
  in World War II, 61
    mine sniffers, *68*, 69, *69*
    uncertain future for pets, 130, 133
    with patrols, 67
  messengers in World War I, 58, *59*, *60*, 60–1
  method of training, 56–8
    R.A.V.C. programme, 70–1
  relationship with handlers, 71
  R.S.P.C.A. advice on wartime feeding, 133
  Russian suicide dogs, 71
  searching out casualties of air raids, 124, 127
  sources of supply for army, 70
  training handlers, 71
Dolphins, 161, 163
Donald (deer mascot, 42nd Royal Highlanders), 146
Donkeys, 154–8
Duffy (donkey), 156
Dunkirk, 102

East African Campaign (1916–17), 154
Eclipse (Household Cavalry horse), 53
Edgehill, Battle of (1642), 18
Edward II, King of England, 16
Edward III, King of England, 18
Edwards, Major T.J., 137, 146
Egypt
  horse-drawn chariots, 13
  relief of Gordon, 84
Eisenhower, General Dwight D., 134
Elephants, 110–19
  as builders of bridges and roads, 116, *116*, 119
  as pack animals, *114*, 115, *115*, 116
  early use in war, 112
  relationship with drivers, 110
  worried by artillery noise, 112
Eritrea, 87
  use of mules, 102
Espionage, use of pigeons in, 76
Experimental animals, 160–1, 163

Fairfax-Blakeborough, Major Jack, 46
Faith (cat), 128–9, *129*
Falcons, 81, 83
Falklands War (1982), 109, 163
  potential use for mine dogs, 70
Feiser, Louis, 161
Flight-Sergeant Lewis (goat mascot, R.A.F.A.), 144, *144*
France
  cavalry in World War II, 51
  use of guard dogs, 61–2
  use of pigeons, 75–6
Franco-Prussian War, fate of wounded horses, 21
Freddie (regimental fox mascot), 143
Frederick the Great, 18–19

Gallipoli, 96, 156
  horse casualties, 40
Galsworthy, John, 28
Gas
  detection by canaries, 83
  effect on horses, 34, *35*
  use of animals in experiments, 160
Germany
  increase in horse numbers between wars, 49
  military dog training, 54
G.I. Joe (pigeon), 79
Gladstone, Hugh S., 76
Gleichen, Lt Count, 86
Glowworms, 163
Goat mascots, 143–5
Gordon, General Charles George, 84
Greece
  cavalry, 15
  use of mules in World War II, 102
Gunpowder, rendering heavy horses obsolete, 18
Gustavus of Sweden, 18

Hannibal, 112
Heraclea, Battle of, 112
Hitler, Adolf, 134
Horse ambulances, 40
Horses, 12–53
  Army Remount Centre, 23
  as status symbols, 18
  Boer War memorial, *162*, 163
  cost of upkeep (1310), 18
  diminishing numbers in England, 28
  docking of tails and ears, 18
  farm work, *132*
  hamstringing, 13, 15
  heavy (*destriers*), 16, 18
  herd instinct, 20
  Hyde Park bombing (1982), 12, *13*
  in Palestine campaign, lacking water, 45
  in World War I, exposure to harsh conditions, 34
  long history of service, 12–13
  police horses in World War II, 129–30, *131*
  requisitioned, 23, 28–30
  shelter from air raids, 122–3
  sixth sense, 129
  vocal cords cut, 106
Huns, saddle introduced by, 15
Hydaspes, Battle of, 15
Hyksos (nomad tribe), 13

Imperial Camel Corps, 84, 86, 92, 94–5, *94*
Inchbald, Geoffrey, 88, 91, 94, 95
Intelligence of animals
  dogs' advance warning of air raids, 128
  exploitation of dolphins, 163
  in elephants, 110
  in horses, distinguishing enemy planes, 34
Irma (dog), 127–8, *127*
Italy, use of mules in World War II, *103*, *104*

Jacob (goose mascot, Coldstream Guards), 136
Jerusalem, assault on (1917), 45–6
Jet (dog), 127, *127*
Jimmy Gray (mule), 109
Judy (dog), 71, 151–2

Kemp, John, 136
Khan (dog mascot, 6th Bn, Cameronians), 152, *152*
Khartoum, 84, 87

Lasocki, Weislaw, 140
Lawrence, T.E., 92
Légion d'Honneur, awarded to pigeon, 75
Lettow, General von, 154
Liddel Hart, Captain Basil, 51
Light Brigade, Charge of, 20
Longbows, 16
Lubow, Robert, 161

Macdonald, Lt.-Col. R.C., *143*
McLellan, A., 71
Macrae, Captain R.A., 102
Magnesia, Battle of (190 B.C.), 112
Mancura, Battle of, 18
Marlborough, John Churchill, 1st Duke of, 18
Marston Moor, Battle of (1644), 134
Mary of Exeter (pigeon), 79, *80*, 80
Mascot Club, *140*, 158
Mascots, 134–53
  variety adopted, 136
  Whale Island Zoo, 140, 145
Matania, Fortunino, 36, *41*
Medals, *see* Croix de Guerre; Dickin Medal; Légion d'Honneur
Mercer, Captain A.C., 20
Metaurus, Battle of (207 B.C.), 112
Mine-sniffing dogs, *68*, *69*, 69
Minnie (pony mascot, Lancashire Fusiliers), 141–3
Mr Bean (mule), 106, 109
Mitchell, Elyre, 46
Mitzi (mule), 106
Mons, 46
Montgomery, Field-Marshal Bernard, 143, *143*
Moreuil Woods, Canadian cavalry charge (1918), 42
Morgan, Geoffrey, 140
Moscow
  last full-scale cavalry charge (1941), 51
  Retreat from (1812), 19
Muldoon, Cpl J., 152, *152*
Mules, 96–109
  as pack animals, *97*, 98, 99
  behaviour, 97–8
  characteristics, 96, 109
  in World War I, 96–101
  in World War II, 102–9
  relationships with drivers, 109
  temperature and disease resistance, 96–7
  vocal cords cut, 106
Munn, Brigadier A.H., 100, 109
Murat, Joachim, 19
Muriel (pig mascot, Royal Inniskillings), 145
Mustard gas, 34

Nail bombs, 53
Napoleon Buonaparte, 19–20
National A.R.P. for Animals Committee, 121
Ney, Marshal Michel, 20
Norman invasion of Britain, 16
Northern Ireland, use of dogs, 70

Olden, Lt.-Col. A.C.N., 46
Olga (police horse), 130, *131*
Oman, use of donkeys in, 158
Omdurman, Battle of (1898), 21
Osman, Captain A.H., 75
Oxen as load pullers, 158–60, *158*, *159*
  in Boer War, *22*

Palestine Campaign (1917–18), 45
  donkeys, 156–7
  fate of cast horses after, 46
  relaxation, 46
  use of camels, *87*, 87–9, *90*, 91
Palestine Campaign (World War II)
  First Cavalry Division formed, 51
  guard dog, 64
  horses hastily shipped out, 49, 51
Parachuting
  by dogs, *66*, 67, 67
  by drugged mules, 106
  sending pigeons to French Resistance, 81
Paris, Siege of (1870), 72
Parrots, warning of approaching aircraft, 76
Peggy (dog), 149–50
Peninsular War, fate of horses retreating from Corunna, 20
People's Dispensary for Sick Animals (P.D.S.A.)
  activities in World War II, 121–2, 124, 127
  care of mascots, 141
  mobile clinics, *120*
  see also Dickin Medal
Peter (dog), 127, *127*, 128
Philip of Macedonia, 15
Pigeons, 72–83
  countered by hawks, 79, 81
  early examples of use, 72
  in World War I, 61, *74*, 75–7
  in World War II, 77–81
  mobile lofts, *74*, 75
  not superseded by wireless, 72
  summoning help for ditched aircraft, 76, 77
  use by USA since World II, 83
  use in espionage, 76
Plumer, Herbert, 25
Poilu (lion mascot, 19th British Division), 140
Poultry, feeding in wartime, 130
Prendys, L/Cpl Peter, 140
Prince (dog), 149
Pyrrhus, 112

Queen's Own Yorkshire Dragoons, 51
Quo Minus (Household Cavalry horse), 53

Rats (dog mascot, Crossmaglen, N.

Ireland), 152, *153*
Rayner, Wing Commander Lea, 80, *81*
Regal (police horse), 130, *131*
Reindeer, 160, *160*
Rex (dog), 127, *127*
Richardson, Lt.-Col. E.H., 54, 57, *58*, 61, 64
Richardson, Mrs E.H., 59
Ricky (mine sniffer dog), 69, *69*, 71
Rip (dog mascot, Poplar A.R.P.), 124, *126*, 127
Rob ('para-dog'), 66, *67*
Robert the Bruce, 16
Roberts, Douglas, 106
Romans, use of horses, 15
Royal Army Veterinary Corps (R.A.V.C.; *formerly* Army Veterinary Corps (*q.v.*)), 40
horse breaking, 51–2
training mine dogs, 70
Royal Horse Artillery, 19, 52, *52*
Royal Society for the Prevention of Cruelty to Animals (R.S.P.C.A.)
activities in World War II, 121–4, 130, 133
advice on feeding dogs in wartime, 133
advice on feeding poultry in wartime, 130
care of mascots, 141
complaints of treatment of horses in Boer War, 27
concern for wounded horses in war, 21
co-operation with A.V.C., 40, 42
provision of horse hospitals in France, 42
Sick and Wounded Horse Fund, 42
Royal Tournament displays, 52
Rupert, Prince, 18, 134
Russians
cavalry in World War II, 51
use of reindeer, 160, *160*
use of suicide dogs, 71

Saddles, 16
camels' pack saddles, 89
for pack mules, 105
introduced by Huns, 15
St Hill Bourne, Dorothea, 79, 129, 136, 141
Salvo (Parachute Regiment dog), 67
Satan (French messenger dog), 60–1
Scientific research, use of animals in, 160–1, 163
Scout (dog mascot, 1st Royal Dragoons), 136–7
Sea gulls, antisubmarine activities, 83
Sealions, 163
Sefton (Household Cavalry horse), 12, *13*, 53, *53*
Sergeant Billy (goat mascot, 5th Canadian Infantry Bn), 144–5
Shellshock in horses, 34
Simon (captain's cat, H.M.S. *Amethyst*), 149, *149*
Simpson, John 156
Slim, Field-Marshal Sir William, 110
Smith, Major-General Frank, 27
Smith, Sydney, 32
Smoky (mule), 109
Somaliland Camel Corps, 87
South Africa
horse casualties (1915), 40
see also Boer War
Special Air Service (S.A.S.), *66*, 67
Spurs, 16
Stirrups, 16
advantages of, 15
Susan (cat mascot of landing craft), 138, *138*
Swords, used with firearms, 18
Syrian Campaign (World War II), 51

Tamblyn, Lt.-Col. D.S., 46
Tanks, superseding calvary horses, 43
Taylor (dog), 128
Thomas, Lowell, 136
Thorn (dog), 127, *127*
Tiny (donkey mascot), *157*
Tirah (donkey mascot, King's Own Yorkshire Light Infantry), 146
Tirpitz (pig mascot, H.M.S. *Glasgow*), 145
Tunisia, use of mules in, 102

Ubique (police horse), 129
Upstart (police horse), 130, *131*

Venus (dog mascot), *147*
Vietnam War
use of mine dogs, 69–70
use of pigeons, 83
Vionville, Battle of (1870), 21
Von Kluck (French messenger dog), 60
Voytek (bear mascot), 140–1

Waterloo, Battle of (1815),
horses in, 20
news of victory by pigeon, 72
Wavell, Archibald Percival, 1st Earl of, *150*
Wellington, Duke of, 136
crossing Bidassoa River, *19*
Whales, 163
Whiskey (cat mascot, H.M.S. *Duke of York*), 138, *138*, 140
William the Conqueror, 16, *17*
Williams, Lt.-Col. D.E., 51
Williams, Frank, 151
Williams, Lt.-Col. J.H., 110, 116–17
Wingate, General Orde, 105, 116
Winkie (pigeon), 77, 79, *79*, *81*
Wolseley, Sir Garnett, 84
Women's Land Army, 130
World War I
camels, 87–95
cavalry activity, 42–3, *43*, 45–6
dogs: as guards, 61
as messengers, 58, *59*, 60, *60*–1
on miscellaneous duties, 62, *62*
source of supply, 54, 56–7
donkeys, 154, 156–8
horses: cast at end of, 46–8, *47*
requisitioned, 28–30, 49
mules, 96–101
pigeons, 74, *74*, 75–7
relationship between horse and rider, 34, 36
role of horses and mules, 30–1, *31*, *32*
terrain difficulties, 32, *33*, 34
training horsemen, 39
veterinary services, 36, *38*, 39, *39*
World War II
animals rescued from bombed buildings, 123–4
British shortage of horses, 49
camels, 87
dogs, 61, 64–5, *64*
effect on 'civilian' animals, 120–33
mules, 102–9
pigeons, 77–81

Zama, Battle of (202 B.C.), 112
Zucha (Russian mine sniffing dog), 69